Journe

'Richard Littledale sees walking as a physical way of knowing the world, oneself, and the spirit that runs through all, but also unpacks it as a powerful metaphor for the steps towards Christian faith. Through personal anecdote, and reference to the writings and observations of others spanning the world and many historical periods, he draws together a case for the walked pilgrimage as the right thing for our times and shows how we might make sense of our lives by living them at walking pace. This is precise, accessible and enjoyable text rather than academic treatise. I look forward to reading more.'

Linda Cracknell, author

'I'm delighted to see *Journey* hit the bookshelves, because it's so desperately needed by Christians today! In a fast-paced, high-tech world, this book invites us to slow down and take the ancient way of the pilgrim. Richard Littledale writes with wit, imagination and heart as he unpacks the metaphor of the Christian life as a pilgrimage, providing a travel guide to help us make this momentous journey our own.

'Put on your walking shoes and pick up *Journey* – a book that will inspire you to leave your spiritual sofa and embark on the way of faith.'

Dr Lisa Deam, medieval scholar, author and speaker

'Life is a journey and the image of pilgrimage is at the heart of the Christian's life and faith. From the origins of the universe and Genesis (the book of beginnings) to the present day, people have been journeying, exploring, seeking and discovering things about the world, themselves and God. The notion of pilgrimage, taking an outward journey to inform and transform the landscape of the heart and the soul, has been prevalent throughout history. Its renaissance in our contemporary culture encourages and illustrates humanity's quest for the divine, a spiritual hunger and a desire for a deeper life.

'Richard's passion for pilgrimage, his knowledge and understanding of the dynamics of taking a journey provide the reader with a great companion on the road. Anyone contemplating a pilgrimage or who wishes to understand more of what "walking with God" might entail would be well served by reading this excellent and inspiring resource.'

Roy Searle; Northumbria Community; Fellow of St John's College, Durham; National Pioneering Consultant, and former President, Baptist Union of Great Britain

'The author helps us to understand walking as a spiritual act. This is a vital insight in a world that might die of over consumption. He shares from his own experience and that of some famous pilgrims. This book can help us to turn our life into a pilgrimage.'

Ray Simpson, Founding Guardian, The International Community of Aidan and Hilda, www.aidanandhilda.org

Journey

The Way of the Disciple

Richard Littledale

Authentic

First published 2017 by Authentic Media Limited,
PO Box 6326, Bletchley, Milton Keynes, MK1 9GG.
authenticmedia.co.uk

British Library Cataloguing in Publication Data

A catalogue record for this book is available from the British Library.

ISBN: 978-1-84227-985-4
978-1-84227-955-7 (e-book)

Unless otherwise stated, Scripture quotations are taken from the Holy Bible, New
International Version Anglicised. Copyright © 1979, 1984, 2011 Biblica. Used
by permission of Hodder & Stoughton Ltd, an Hachette UK company. All rights
reserved. 'NIV' is a registered trademark of Biblica UK trademark number 1448790.

Extracts marked cev are from the Contemporary English Version® Copyright
© 1995 American Bible Society. All rights reserved. Anglicized edition
© 2000HarperCollins*Publishers*.

Scripture quotations marked (esv) are from The Holy Bible, English Standard
Version* (ESV*), copyright © 2001 by Crossway. Used by permission. All rights
reserved.

Scripture quotations marked (gnt) are from the Good News Bible © 1994 published
by the Bible Societies/HarperCollins Publishers Ltd UK, Good News Bible ©
American Bible Society 1966, 1971, 1976, 1992. Used with permission.

Cover image: *The Pilgrim*. Sculpture and photograph
by Glenn Morris glennmorris.co.uk

Cover design by David Smart smartsart.co.uk
Printed and bound by CPI Group (UK) Ltd., Croydon, CR0 4YY

To all who have served alongside
me as fellow travellers,
with my heartfelt thanks

Contents

Foreword

Everyone, it seems, is on a journey. When non-league football teams get the draw for the first round of the FA Cup, the sports journalists write about the start of 'the road to Wembley'. When celebrities learn to dance for Saturday night TV, they keep a diary of their Strictly Come Dancing 'journey'. We shouldn't be surprised. Life is a journey from infancy to adulthood (and a second half we're less keen to talk about, though this book does). Christian faith is also a journey, from the Garden of Eden to the new Jerusalem, from birth to resurrection, and frequently described in both parts of our Bible as walking with God.

The Community of Aidan and Hilda, to which I belong, describes itself as 'a people who journey with God', inspired by those great wanderers for the love of God, the Celtic saints. It's about time somebody dedicated a whole book to journeying in this sense, and that's exactly what Richard Littledale has done. He shows how physically going on pilgrimage has historically been part of Christian spirituality, introduces us in vivid closeness to the pilgrims of past centuries, and then shows us how we can all be pilgrims in our discipleship today.

Pilgrimage, whether Christian or as an expression of a less defined spiritual journey, is enjoying a renewed popularity as new routes are devised and waymarked. This book might well inspire you to try one out. In 2013 I set out to backpack the St Cuthbert Way from Melrose to Lindisfarne. An injury cut short my journey but even in two days I encountered God in fresh and unexpected ways. But for many of us, our life circumstances may mean that we may never be able to go on a pilgrimage even if we want to. If pilgrimage is the focusing in a specialized way of the journey of life, is there some other way of accessing its benefits without actually leaving home? This is precisely what this book allows us to do. Richard invites us to reflect on what leaving home, taking provisions, making communications, finding companions, coping with distractions, and coming to our journey's end mean in our day-to-day lives. He also introduces us to some of the new expressions of Christian life and community, like my own, which are trying to live these insights in our daily walk as disciples of Jesus.

Richard is himself the embodiment of what this book is all about. He admits that he has never been on a pilgrimage himself and has only experienced it through others. The fact that he can write about it so insightfully, and in a way that is so rooted in the stuff of everyday life, is proof of what this book sets out to do – to help us all to journey with God, and to travel well.

Simon Reed
Joint Guardian, The Community of
Aidan and Hilda

Preface

Are you the kind of person who cannot work without a view? It doesn't have to be much of a view – just so long as there is a glimpse of greenery, or even just of the sky. Are you the kind of person who feels trapped unless there is some tiny hint of a further horizon? People who feel that way are not necessarily adventurers. They are not about to drop everything at any minute and circumnavigate the globe. I know that for a fact, because I am one of them. I would never call myself an adventurer of any kind, and yet I am plagued by the siren call of distance. I am inspired by the far horizon and lured by the prospect of what is over the next hill or around the next corner. Much of this book has been written in unfamiliar places, and I often find that my thoughts flow best when my body is in motion. Linda Cracknell, author of *Doubling Back: Ten Paths Trodden in Memory*, clearly feels the same: 'It's as if I think better on the move, think more creatively, or as Jean-Jacques Rousseau would have it, "my mind only works with my legs". Slow but alert. Attentive to both inner and outer landscapes.'[1]

I love to write when gazing out of a train window at the landscape slipping by. Somehow the lack of physical anchor frees the thoughts to run free as well. Inner and outer journeys, like physical and mental freedom, are inextricably linked. To find the motif of journey running so deeply in Scripture and church history has been a great joy to me. To sense that pilgrims, both contemporary and medieval, might have something to say to a person looking out of the window of a speeding train has been a real pleasure. To sense that the idea of journey runs so deep in Christian faith and tradition has been a revelation.

The pages which follow have been enhanced by illustrations, both without and within. The photo which adorns the cover came into my possession on Wednesday 11 February 2015. On that day I visited the remains of a Cistercian monastery in Strata Florida (Floral Valley) in Ceredigion, Wales. Over 900 years earlier it had been visited by the Archbishop of Canterbury's envoy, Gerald of Wales: 'We reached Strata Florida that night and stayed there for a while. From there we journeyed on, leaving on our right the lofty mountains of Moruge, called Elenydd in Welsh.'[2] High above the monastery when I visited could be seen a giant figure striding across the landscape. I took a few rather disappointing photos, made some enquiries, and discovered that the huge sculpture, made out of railway sleepers, had been made by Welsh sculptor Glenn Morris. It was called *Pilgrim* and formed part of a series of exhibits in response to the monastery's past. The artist described this particular work as 'a figure toiling against the weather, rugged landscape (and perhaps life . . .)'. He also said he loved the idea of people coming across it 'almost by chance' – exactly as I had done.[3] The photo has been kindly donated by the artist.

The line drawings have been donated too, by artists near and far:

- Max Ellis – a photographer and illustrator, working on everything from majestic photographs of stags to caricatures of musicians

- Ryan Cartwright – a computer worker by day and an illustrator and children's book author by night
- Ashley Fitzgerald – a multimedia artist whose Jewish roots and personal experiences inform his art
- Rachel Morris – an artist and illustrator living in Teddington
- Danielle Somerfield – an independent graphic designer and artist
- Maureen Kerr – an illustrator currently working as a cook at the army base on the island of St Kilda.

Like pilgrims joining me on the journey, they have fallen in step with me as I have written, and offered their artworks for free. Unlike most books, you will find that there is no unifying style to the illustrations. Each one is as individual as the artist who created it. This is deliberate, though. Pilgrimage is a journey walked together, and part of its joy is the diversity of our companions.

If you are up for a journey, why not turn the page?

Acknowledgements

Glenn Morris – for his kind permission to use the image of his magnificent *Pilgrim* sculpture on the cover

Ryan Cartwright, Max Ellis, Ashley Fitzgerald, Maureen Kerr, Rachel Morris and Danielle Somerfield – for their kindly donated illustrations

Danny Konz, Penelope Swithinbank and Sue Culver – for their contributions around the campfire

Helen Rees – for her help with researching the 'tale of a shell'

Mike Parsons – for his gentle wisdom and editorial input

Fiona Littledale – for finding *Sightseers into Pilgrims* and so many things besides

Author's Note

In Chapter 11, the author creates an imaginary scenario in which six real-life pilgrims from various historical periods and backgrounds meet around a campfire and strike up a conversation. The speeches are partly quotations from medieval and present-day sources, and partly fictional. To avoid hindering the flow of the conversation, no notes are provided in the text. Following is a list of the quotations and their sources:

Geoffrey Chaucer

'Thanne longen folk to goon on pilgrimages, / And palmeres
   for to seken straunge strondes, / To ferne halwes, kowthe in
   sondry londes; / And specially from every shires ende / Of
   Engelond to Caunterbury they wende . . .'
Canterbury Tales (Kindle, 2007), General Prologue, lines 12–16.

Margery Kempe

'When I was commanded to go, I could in no way withstand it.'
The Book of Margery Kempe (London: Penguin, 2005), loc. 3877.

'Show you are truly God, and no evil spirit, that has brought me here into the perils of the sea, whose counsel I have trusted and followed for many years, and shall do, through your mercy, if you deliver us from out of these grievous perils.'
The Book of Margery Kempe, loc. 4130.

'with all my heart . . . just as he had brought me to see this earthly city of Jerusalem, so he would give me grace to see the blissful city of Jerusalem above, the city of heaven'
The Book of Margery Kempe, loc. 1579.

Aymeric Picaud

'divinely illuminated by paradisiac carbuncles, constantly honoured by divine fragrances, radiant in the light of celestial candles and devoutly attended by watching angels'
Cited in *The Pilgrim's Guide: A 12th Century Guide for the Pilgrim to St James of Compostela* (ed. James Hogarth; London: Confraternity of St James, 1996), p. 77.

'whosoever receives them and gives them hospitality has for his guest not only St James but our Lord himself'
Cited in *The Pilgrim's Guide*, p. 87.

Sue

Sue's comments throughout
Email to the author, 30 January 2015.

Penelope

Penelope's comments throughout
Email to the author, 12 November 2014.

Dean

'walking in the footsteps of those saints of old'
Cited from Digipilgrim blog https://www.youtube.com/
watch?v=9dkZLA1s4J0 (accessed 25 Nov. 2015).

Stand at the crossroads and look;
ask for the ancient paths,
ask where the good way is, and walk in it,
and you will find rest for your souls.
Jeremiah 6:16

Journey by Max Ellis

1

Journey: An Introduction

*Do nothing in haste; look well to each step; and
from the beginning think what may be the end.*

These are the words of Edward Whymper, the Victorian mountaineer who was the first European to climb the Matterhorn.
Though written well over a century ago, they still ring true –
and not just when it comes to climbing. Our Christian life is
lived one step at a time, neither more nor less. I have been a
Christian for over thirty years and for most of them I have been
unable to sing the words of Frances Ridley Havergal's hymn
'Take my life and let it be' without a smile:

Take my feet and let them be
Swift and beautiful for thee . . .[1]

My feet will never be swift or beautiful. However, as a pastor
it has fallen to me to act as a kind of spiritual courier, guiding
people from the plains of unbelief into the foothills of faith, and
pointing out the path to the higher slopes of God's goodness.
As I have done this, I have become more and more convinced
that this is a journey made on foot – step, by step, by step.

Steps, of course, are so basic that we don't even have to think about them. From the day we get up off our bottoms and toddle our first upright steps, we never give them another thought. Every step is, in fact, a fall caught just in time. As we walk we transfer our body weight forwards, with the front leg bearing the weight. As that front foot strikes the ground, so the knee bends slightly with the impact, bringing the rest of the body almost to the point of overbalancing. This triggers a response by the nervous system, telling the trailing foot to come around and take the strain in order to avert disaster. With that done, the whole cycle begins again and so we propel ourselves across the earth's surface. On a good day we may perform that cycle of actions over 10,000 times, whether around our place of work or across the wild earth.

To make any journey on foot is countercultural in a world where speed is of the essence, and a person may be isolated from their global neighbours by the relative speed of their broadband connection. Few of us walk to work, and walking as a leisure pastime has become part of an expensive and highly technical outdoor sports industry. The idea of a long walk which seems more about the journey than the destination seems alien to our driven and performance-oriented society. Setting out on his journey on foot, journalist Jack Hitt commented that: 'What the modern pilgrim is exiled from is not a place but velocity. I haven't left the world of the city; I have left the realm of the car. What distinguishes me is not that I am out of town but that I am on foot.'[2]

In recent years there has been a marked resurgence in the appetite among Christians and 'spiritual enquirers' of every hue for pilgrimage. In 1985, for instance, 491 people received a certificate of completion on the pilgrim route, or *Camino*, to Santiago de Compostela. In 2010 the number was over

270,000. Among those thousands not all are Christians, or even religious. Some walk for the physical benefits, some walk to unravel the threads of a complicated past, and others look for some form of enlightenment. Often it is the journey itself, rather than the destination, which seems to matter most. This is a kind of mobile therapy, where the knots of a tangled and complex life can be unravelled as the miles roll beneath the walker's feet. Whatever their reasons, ancient pilgrimage routes such as the Camino de Santiago now bear more modern footprints than at any point in my lifetime. This seems like a good time to consider the Christian life as a journey lived at walking pace.

To say that the Christian life is 'just' lived at walking pace, though, makes it sound like an easy thing – as if we can just saunter our way from first calling to heavenly arrival without even breaking a sweat. Anyone who has ever travelled a substantial distance on foot will know that it is not so. In his youth my father was a very keen walker, travelling great distances between youth hostels with his canvas knapsack on his back. Years later, when my brother and I came along, he was still keen to walk. With our much shorter legs we often found it hard to keep up. What was a pleasant stroll to him often felt like more of a route march to us, and I frequently struggled at the back. Realizing this, he took me on one side and explained that the secret to enjoying a long walk was not to concentrate on the distance, but on the contents. In other words, it was better to savour the sights and sounds as you passed through, rather than spending the whole journey thinking about its end. In this way, the miles passed more quickly and the journey was a whole lot more pleasant. It is in such a spirit that I write the following chapters.

In them I want to drill deep down into the motif of journey and pilgrimage which lies at the heart of Christian belief. I hope you will find the walk through these pages worth your while, and that you will enjoy the sights and sounds along the way rather than being consumed with the desire to get to the end!

Faith in Motion

Leaving my childhood walks with Dad on one side, the story of this book begins on a hot August afternoon several years ago in northern Brittany. En route (by car!) from one pretty town to another, we stopped at the little harbour of Port à la Duc. In fact, to call it a harbour would be to exaggerate. It had formerly been a small harbour, but now the inlet had silted up so much that it was little more than a trickle. On the other side of the road from the inlet was a small string of pretty cottages, and I stopped to take some photos. It was then that I noticed a narrow grassy path leading up past the cottages and over a small hill before disappearing out of sight. Beside it was a noticeboard, its paint peeling in the salty air, with a picture of a Templar on it. The sign explained that Port à la Duc was once an important point on the pilgrim trail. In centuries gone by, people would cross from Weymouth by rowing boat, disembark at this tiny port, and then begin the long trek of almost 1,000 miles to Santiago de Compostela. My mind reeled at the thought of it. Here were people who had rarely even left their villages crossing the ocean and embarking on this gargantuan journey. Along the way they would be reliant upon the protection of the Templars (as depicted on the sign), the kindness of strangers and the companionship of each other. They would face hunger, exhaustion and possibly disease – not to mention the fact that they would be strangers in a foreign land and unable to speak the language. Why, why would they do it?

The thing is, journeys are not a new thing for people of faith. Before the route to Santiago, there were other pilgrims crossing vast distances to places like Rome or Jerusalem. Before that there was the apostle Paul, forever on the move from city to city and town to town until Roman captivity finally obliged him to stay in one place. Centuries before that, there were Ruth and her sister Orpah, setting out with their mother-in-law for a strange land. In the end, Orpah turned back, but Ruth made the journey, and in doing so walked into the ancestral line of Jesus. Before that there was the patriarch Jacob restlessly moving on from place to place, and before him his father Abraham – tipped out of his comfort zone at the age of 70 and told by God to pack his bags. Abraham would be followed several generations later by Moses, whose journey motif would help to shape Judeo-Christian theology forevermore. His exodus journey from slavery to freedom via adversity would provide inspiration for many, both inside and outside the Christian faith. His journey would be recast by black slaves in search of freedom in America, oppressed peoples in apartheid South Africa, and many others since.

The fledgling Christian church became almost instantly a journeying community. The early martyrdom of Stephen meant that many had to flee from Jerusalem for their lives. They took their new faith with them, and passed it on as they travelled across borders and oceans. What started as an accidental expansion then became an intentional journey of mission. Anyone who has ever owned a Bible with a set of New Testament maps in the back will know from all those dotted lines that the apostle Paul, at least, was rarely in one place for long. After him would come others who would carry the gospel to parts of the world of which he had never heard. Irish monks in coracles, priests in sailing ships, pastors on motorbikes and missionaries in light aircraft would continue what Paul had started.

Our understandings of Christian pilgrimage can be traced back a very long way. We should probably go back all the way to Constantine's mother, Helena Augusta, in the third century. While her son was busy using military might to establish a kind of Christendom, she was taking the first steps in what began to be known as pilgrimage. With her son's influence behind her and his military might to protect her, she began to travel around the Holy Land. Wherever she could identify sites which had played an important part in the life of Christ, she had churches built. She also became the first serious collector of relics, from fragments of the 'true cross' to bones of the early apostles. As the centuries went by, many of these relics found their way across Europe, and began to draw pilgrims by their thousands. Here were people drawn to something which bore some relation to someone who had been touched by the divine – and they wanted some of it.

In the early stages of writing and researching this book, I paid a visit to the cathedral in Cologne. The twin towers of this magnificent building, still blackened by smoke damage from the Second World War, soar some 157 metres above the modern city below. In the heart of the cathedral, inside the biggest golden reliquary in Western Europe, are said to lie the bones of the magi who once visited Christ. In centuries past they had gone from Constantinople to Milan, and then on to Cologne. If the provenance is true, then a visitor like me can press his nose, or his face, up to the iron railings around the reliquary and be within touching distance of the remains of someone who once knelt at the bedside of the infant Christ. These great pilgrimage sites became like magnets to the faithful, summoning them from far and near to make a connection between the physical world and their heartfelt faith.

The six most important pilgrimage sites were as follows:

- **Jerusalem**, where the Church of the Holy Sepulchre was said to contain the original burial place of Christ; pilgrims could also visit the remaining wall of Solomon's original temple
- **Rome**, where the Basilica of St Peter contained the relics of Saints Peter and Paul
- **Cologne**, where the bones of the magi were said to reside in a golden casket in the cathedral
- **Boulogne**, where the Basilica of Notre Dame contained a glowing statue of the Virgin Mary which had appeared miraculously in a boat floating in the estuary of the river
- **Santiago de Compostela**, where the body of St James was buried
- **Canterbury**, burial site of St Thomas Beckett.

So great were the numbers travelling to these sites that they were required to adopt a certain style of dress in order that they could be identified as pilgrims. In this way, they were subject to a 'pilgrim's code' rather than the specific laws of each country through which they passed. This code was the forerunner of our understanding of international law today.

By the time the Reformation came along, pilgrimage was big business for some. The poor, kept in fear of God by their priests, were frightened into taking pilgrimages which they could ill afford. People who had rarely left their county, or even their village, were criss-crossing Europe in the hopes of buying some eternal gain. Martin Luther wanted to see an end to the practice, declaring, 'Pilgrimages should be stopped. There is no good in them; no commandment enjoins them; and no obedience attaches to them.'[3] Pilgrimages began to wane in popularity, with some still making more 'localized' ones. In Great Britain, for example, pilgrimages to Walsingham, Canterbury, Lindisfarne, Winchester and Holy Wells continued. Some of those sites still retain their pilgrimage 'status' today. People seek them out in search of enlightenment, disentanglement from their complex lives, peace or even healing. There is a church in Ceredigion, Mid Wales, which nestles in the crook of a mountain at Ysbyty Cynfyn. It once stood on the pilgrim route from North Wales down to St David's. (In its heyday three pilgrimages to St David's were deemed to be the equal of one to Jerusalem.) The church still bears the scallop-shell emblem on its gate – a reminder of a time centuries ago when weary pilgrims could stop at the hostel which once stood here and ask for food and shelter from the Knights Hospitaller who ran it. The knights are long gone, and the church is now locked during the week, but the churchyard bears witness to a much older time and place, ringed by standing stones which once marked a place of pre-Christian worship. This strange and lovely place is a symbol of the complex context in which pilgrimage is understood today.

Most of us live in multi-ethnic and multi-faith societies where pilgrimage means many things to many people. In some places, the more ancient roots of pilgrimage have been lost among other things. On a visit to Canterbury Cathedral, once the most important site of pilgrimage in the United Kingdom, I was unsure whether to laugh or cry when seeing a small book about pilgrimage on the gift-shop counter, all but obscured by plastic ducks dressed as bishops!

The rediscovery of pilgrimages abroad from the United Kingdom may well owe their origins to a cabinet-maker from Loughborough. On 9 June 1841, 32-year-old Thomas Cook was walking from his home in Market Harborough to a temperance meeting in Leicester. Reflecting on the destructive social effects of poor education and cheap alcohol, he had something of a revelation. He later recalled, 'The thought suddenly flashed across my mind as to the practicability of employing the great powers of railways and locomotion for the furtherance of social reform.'[4] The following month he organized his first ever railway-tour, and his travel company was born. Affordable holidays for the masses became his watchword, and he organized many such trips within Britain. In 1855 he took his first trip to continental Europe, travelling from Harwich to Paris via Antwerp. Trips to Switzerland and Italy were to follow. He became more and more adventurous, and in 1869 took his first tour to the Holy Land, which he described as 'the greatest event of my tourist life'.[5] Many would follow his lead.

Today people who can afford it think nothing of jetting off to the other side of the world, and we see holidays as a right. Pilgrimages, though, are not holidays. In an age of deep scepticism about the apparent certainties of organized religion, there is a keen appetite for spiritual connection. Cathedral worship is burgeoning as never before, and people are taking pilgrimages again. Jack Hitt, a self-confessed atheist, has written a best-seller about his journey on the Santiago pilgrimage. Martin Sheen has toured America with a film on the same subject, talking about discipleship as the reason we were made. Even sceptical British journalist Peter Stanford has swallowed his pride and written *The Extra Mile: A 21st Century Pilgrimage*. What is going on?

Thought in Motion

To make any journey on foot is countercultural in a world where we are ruled by our watches and time is too precious to waste. However, it is that very driven culture which has led to people leaving the tablet at home and taking to the pilgrim's road. Kosuke Koyama was born in Tokyo in 1929, but spent most of his life in the United States. A theologian of enormous renown, he placed great emphasis on simplicity. Writing in what seems like an age of technological innocence in the 1970s, he warned about the mixed blessing of technology: 'Technology is like a fire. It can cook rice for our enjoyment and nutrition, and it can also reduce our house to ashes . . . How much technology can we use without being victimized by the technological Maya?'[6] (Here *Maya* means 'illusion'.)

Koyama's best-known work is his book *Three Mile an Hour God*. The curious title was born of the idea that the God of the Bible has always been experienced 'on the move', but that the moving was at walking pace, rather than anything quicker. Unlike followers of other religions, Jews and Christians did not carry their gods with them as they travelled; rather God himself travelled with them. The thing is, we struggle to notice him when we travel too quickly.

Although I am writing this now at a desk overlooking my garden, most of it has been conceived while travelling. Gazing out of train windows, watching the rain run down a strange hotel window, passing through a different landscape – these are the places where creativity flows. I had initially thought that this was a peculiar oddity of mine. However, discussions with other creative people reveal the same: our thoughts are often freed when we are on the move. In her book *Wanderlust*, Rebecca Solnit says that there are reasons for this: 'Walking is the intentional act closest to the unwilled rhythms of the body . . . a state in which the mind, the body and the world are aligned as though they were three characters finally in conversation together, three notes suddenly making a chord.'[7] Taking her thoughts further, archaeologists have discovered that *walking* through a historical landscape with those whose forebears have lived there may release surprising insights about its past inaccessible through other means. Perhaps this is why Nietzsche claimed that 'all truly great thoughts are conceived by walking'.[8] Writer Linda Cracknell says that 'it's as if I think better on the move, think more creatively'. She goes on to describe this walking while thinking as 'slow but alert. Attentive to both inner and outer landscapes'. [9]

A friend of mine works for a national organization committed to getting people out on their two feet to enjoy the countryside. As you would expect, he is something of an evangelist for walking. Who could blame him? It has been said that if there were a drug which conferred all the benefits of daily gentle exercise it would be the most popular and most expensive on the market. In short, walking is good for us. However, it is not just good for our limbs and our circulatory systems. It is good for our brains and our emotions too. It will come as no surprise to some reading this that men are not always good at talking to each other. Stick them either side of a pub table with a pint in their hands and they might just manage it, but conversations with their family may be a bridge too far. Get them out in the countryside, though, walking along and looking forward rather than at each other, and it is a different thing altogether. No wonder my friend goes to work each day with a spring in his step. He may not only be preserving the countryside for generations to come; he may well be preserving those generations too!

When we walk, we think, we create, we interact and we talk. What could be a better aid to faith than this?

To Be a Pilgrim

Whichever route we take, and whether we travel within our own country or cross borders on the way to our spiritual goal, there are certain elements which are axiomatic to the pilgrim's journey:

- **Leaving home**. At some point, after all the planning, praying and preparation, the pilgrim must leave home. His or her parting may be marked by something as solemn as a mass or as simple as a family meal – but leaving home is a must. The point will come where they must round the first corner which deprives them of the sight of home. Ahead lies the journey, and, with each step, home with its familiar smells, sounds and rhythms falls further behind. In the early days of the journey, homesickness and longing may be a real problem. As the journey passes its midpoint, this homesickness may turn into a different kind of longing altogether – a longing for the home which is to come.
- **Discomfiture** is a feature of any journey of substantial length. This may take many forms. In the early stages of the journey it may be physical, as the soles of the feet and the muscles of the legs grow accustomed to the novel demands being made of them. I mentioned earlier the meteoric rise in the popularity of the ancient pilgrimage route from different points in Europe to the cathedral of Santiago de Compostela. This route has been greatly popularized in recent years as different writers have undertaken it. It received a significant boost in 2010 with the launch of Emilio Estevez' film *The Way*. The glorious cinematography and appealing plot have fooled many, though. The Camino is much more than a long walk, and should not be undertaken lightly. Blistered

feet and damaged tendons are part of the price any pilgrim must pay. Over time, as the body grows used to these demands, discomfiture of another kind may take over. The pilgrim is in a strange place now. The places through which he or she is passing look different; the people eat different food and speak a different tongue. In short, the pilgrim does not belong here – and that will continue to be the case until journey's end.

- **Dependence**. As the pilgrim passes through these strange places, she or he will have to rely for provision on those to whom the territory belongs. It simply is not possible to carry everything for the journey with you, and therefore provision from strangers along the way is an inescapable element of pilgrimage. This may be everything from a cooling drink or a simple meal to the provision of medical care. There is now a rich tradition of hospitality and provision for pilgrims, which encompasses everything from Crusader forts on the roads into Jerusalem to small bed-and-breakfast houses in central Spain.

- **Companions**. Of course pilgrims will be reliant not only on those whose houses they pass, but those who pass with them. Every account of pilgrimage, from the *Canterbury Tales* to Jack Hitt's *Off the Road*, describes the relationships which are forged between pilgrims as they travel. These people may be rougher, or softer, than you. They may seem overly vulgar or unduly refined. They may get up when you want to lie in, or go to bed when you want to stay up. Their habits may be annoying, their dress sense embarrassing, and the sound of their voices anything from reassuring to enervating – but you are stuck with them, and they with you.

- **Provisions**. Although the pilgrim is dependent upon strangers for daily provision, there will be some things which she or he chooses to carry from beginning to end. What will they be? For the early pilgrims they were little more than a cloak and hat for protection, a staff for support, a gourd for carrying water, and a 'scrip' or small pack to carry a little food. A pilgrim is a person who has taken tough decisions about which few things *must* come on the journey and the many things which *may* be left behind.

- **Uncertainty** is an inevitable element of any kind of travel. This may take the form of uncertainty about the road itself, or about the people and places you encounter along it. When home is far behind, and journey's end is impossibly far away, an uncertainty may creep in about whether the journey itself is doable. From this it is a short step to worrying about the reasons for going in the first place and your ability to complete the journey. Uncertainty and adventure are two sides of the same coin. The scent of adventure may be what made us start on the journey in the first place, but sometimes adventure and danger smell very similar.

- **Journey's end**. Every journey must, by definition, have an end. A pilgrimage is not a circular route but a journey from home to an unfamiliar place with a spiritual objective. At some point that objective will be reached.

All these things are descriptions of pilgrimage, but they should be descriptions of discipleship itself. Disciples, at least initially, were those instructed to leave their homes, depart with only the barest essentials to carry, and proceed on a journey which Christ would set out for them. Jesus instructed his disciples to 'take nothing for the journey except a staff – no bread, no bag, no money in your belts' (Mark 6:8). Along the way they would lean on each other, expect miraculous provision and protection, and come at last to their goal. Atheist Peter Stanford, in his honest and delightful book *The Extra Mile*, expresses it like this: 'The very act of going on pilgrimage might be seen as making the body do what the soul desires.'[10]

Pilgrimage, it would seem, is worth another look . . .

For Reflection

Each chapter will be provided with a few pointers for reflection on the subjects covered. Think of it as the best window-seat on the train – the countryside slipping away beside you as you think about what you have seen. Think of it as the patch of soft grass at the top of the hill you have just climbed – a place to take a breather and take in the view. This is your opportunity to stop and think for a while, laying the pilgrim's staff and rucksack on one side, before you continue the journey . . .

1. Have you ever been on any kind of pilgrimage?
2. Linda Cracknell says that 'in a sense, any long walk is a pilgrimage'. Do you agree, and if not, why?
3. What do you hope to learn, or gain, on your journey through these pages?

Leaving Home by Ryan Cartwright

2

Leaving Home

Writing some five hundred years before the birth of Christ, Lao Tzu, archivist at the imperial library in China, wrote that 'the journey of a thousand miles begins with a single step'.[1] He ought to know – at the age of 80 he set out to walk all the way from the palace in Beijing to the border with Tibet. In my experience the journey of a thousand miles often begins with turning the car around and heading back home to check that I have locked the front door! After that, since I have stopped anyway, I find myself checking that the picnic is in the boot, the car is fully fuelled, and my printed directions are near to hand. In truth, the start of any journey is wreathed with all manner of emotions, both positive and negative.

On the one hand, we are looking forward to encountering new horizons and taking in new sights along the way. On the other, we may be worried about leaving our home unattended. We may be concerned for the property itself, for dependents for whom we care, or even for pets we leave behind. As we travel to the airport or railway station, we may find ourselves looking forward to the experience of travelling itself; but then again, if the journey is a long one, we may be plagued by the knowledge that we will be in severe discomfort before journey's end. Unless we can afford to pay for the best of the best at every stage, this is almost inevitable. Occasionally we can experience a kind of advance nostalgia, already pining for those familiar sights and faces which we have not yet left behind. The emotional adjustment necessary to begin any journey is not a simple one.

Furthermore, there are all the practical arrangements to be made. I have recently taken my first ever package holiday, and was amazed to find that the company provided an online 'checklist' for all the jobs which needed to be done. For years I had written such things on little scraps of paper or backs of envelopes, but essentially it is the same list. Deliveries to the house need to be cancelled, appliances shut down, bills paid off, and doors and windows locked. Before all that can take place, there may have been a long process of buying appropriate clothing and equipment, washing clothes, buying provisions, converting currency and packing luggage. Furthermore, if the journey is to more exotic places abroad we may need to undertake all kinds of inoculations before we can set off. I used to be petrified of injections, but ever since they have become associated in my mind with foreign travel I find them easier to bear. There is also the whole business of insurance to consider, since nobody wants their journey blighted by enormous medical bills or luggage which is lost forever and cannot be replaced.

Of course in the heyday of medieval pilgrimage inoculations were unheard of, and our modern forms of transport were unimaginable. That is not to say, however, that the process of leaving home for pilgrimage was any less complicated. If a subsistence farmer were to leave home for several months, arrangements would have to be made about who would tend his land lest it go to ruin. For the most part, it would only be the males in the family who left on pilgrimage, and before the man went, a visit to the local priest would be in order. The priest would not only bless the departure, but also witness the sealing of an oath regarding how long his wife should wait, in the case of his failure to return, before marrying again. This may seem unduly melodramatic to us, but in an age where a single woman was acutely vulnerable to poverty and destitution the perils of the journey meant that such things had to be considered. Bags packed, farewells made and responsibilities handed over, the pilgrim would often gather with others from his diocese to receive a bishop's blessing before heading to the coast and the start of the pilgrim's journey. Such services were a rite of passage, both for the pilgrims leaving, and for those they would leave behind. Today some of the 'Friends of the Camino' do a similar thing, with the Alicante branch holding a church service for all those departing on the Camino, followed by a farewell meal.

Anyone making a journey, whether near or far, and for sacred or secular purpose, will appreciate this one truth: you cannot begin a journey without first leaving home. Not only that, but the act of 'leaving' may be far more than physical. A journey involves not just making that first step of Tzu's one thousand miles, but also untwisting the strands of thought, emotion and habit which are entwined about wherever we call home. The icon for 'home' is now universally recognized around the world. On an unfamiliar desktop or device it provides a reassuring point of familiar reference. However, our understandings of what 'home' means away from the computer screen may be hugely different from each other. 'Home' can describe anything from a physical location to a set of habits or a style of cooking. People like to simplify this by saying that 'home is where the heart is', but it really is not that simple. Home may describe a way of thinking, an unwritten set of cultural expectations, a sense of propriety, a network of personal connections, or a centre of gravity to our lives. Whatever we mean by 'home', leaving it behind is no small thing.

Biblical Journeys

The Bible is brimming over with stories of people travelling on journeys of faith. Some travel far from home across borders and oceans, while others travel only from one village or town to the next. Whatever kind of journey they take, no secret is made of the wrench which must signal its start. At the start of his journey, Abram is left in no doubt about the costs involved. God instructs him that he is to leave 'your country, your people and your father's household' (Genesis 12:1) – three of the most important anchors in any Middle Eastern life. For the ancient peoples of the Near East, the relationship with the land was an emotional and spiritual one, since it represented not just where they lived but where they were 'from'. On my first visit to the United States I was surprised to be asked on more than one occasion where I was 'raised'. However, people ask it because it helps them to make sense of the values and feel of the place which shaped you. For Abram to leave his people behind meant leaving those people who dressed like him, thought like him, ate like him and behaved like him. Although he takes his wife and immediate family with him, to leave his father's household meant to leave behind the protection and status which it afforded him. Ahead lies a long and arduous journey beset with triumph and failure, fear and faith – but it cannot commence until Abram leaves these things behind.

Hagar is another one who makes a journey far from home. After agreeing to bear Abraham's child, she finds herself entangled in a marital dispute between him and his wife, Sarah. Sarah insists that Abraham himself should be the one to throw her out, and so he does. Hagar and her son Ishmael cut very sorry figures in Genesis 21 as Abraham loads them up with a little food and water and sends them off into the desert to fend for themselves. Her way will never return to Abraham, but she and Ishmael will experience God's miraculous provision on the desert road.

We often think of Moses' as the most famous journey in the Old Testament. We would probably think of it as beginning with his encounter at the burning bush. However, in truth it had begun many years earlier. One day he left the royal palace, saw the suffering of his own people, struck down and killed a slave-master, and instantly became a wanted man. In haste he left the palace and all its finery behind, fleeing for his life to the relative safety of Midian. It was this short flight to Midian which prefigured the much longer journey of the exodus. Redacting the story centuries later, the writer of Hebrews wrote that Moses 'refused to be known as the son of Pharaoh's daughter. He chose to be ill-treated along with the people of God rather than to enjoy the fleeting pleasures of sin' (Hebrews 11:24–25). However you see it, Moses' journey had begun by irrevocably leaving home. Whether we see it as a choice or an irrevocable command, this step away from palace and privilege would be one with irreversible consequences for him.

Centuries later, the great prophet Elijah was coming towards the end of his ministry. Kings and queens had shuddered under the blows delivered by his inspired tongue, but now it was time to hand over to the next man. Arriving on the farm of a young man named Elisha, he threw his cloak about the youth's shoulders, thereby signalling his passing on of the baton. This poetic gesture was followed by something far more concrete and irrevocable. Elisha the farmer was set to become a prophet, and he signalled this by making a bonfire of his farming equipment and burning his tractor (in fact, his oxen) on the top. To do so was the most dramatic means imaginable of signalling his intention to leave and never to look back. Long before the phrase about 'burning bridges' was coined, that is exactly what Elisha was doing. Not only that, but the act was sealed by the presence of witnesses. The resulting cooked meat was passed out to the crowd of witnesses gathered to watch the spectacle, and Elisha 'set out to follow Elijah' (1 Kings 19:21).

The Old Testament story of Ruth is pivotal in the unfolding drama of salvation. At its conclusion it will bring about the birth of Jesse, grandfather to King David himself and establishing the royal line of Christ. However, it is easy for the happy ending to eclipse the fact that three women start out on a brave journey of faith in Ruth chapter 1, but only two complete it. Despite joining Ruth in pledging that she would accompany Naomi all the way to journey's end – 'We will go back with you to your people' (Ruth 1:10) – Orpah is unable to go through with it. Some years ago I preached a narrative sermon on the respective journeys of Ruth and Orpah. That sermon would prove to be a milestone in one man's life, as it played a major part in his call to serve God overseas. Remembering the occasion, he wrote to me that:

> when you preached this sermon a heart-wrenching conviction, which I can only attribute to the Holy Spirit, grabbed me and wouldn't let me go. The staff of the good shepherd had struck me and it smarted. Recognition of who God is; obedience; love and loyalty matter in the story of Ruth. We didn't want to end up like Orpah – a nobody with no contribution to God's kingdom.[2]

The story of Ruth's (and Orpah's) journey is a warning to all who would begin the journey of faith that leaving home for unfamiliar faces and places is no small thing, and should not be undertaken lightly.

When Jesus starts to gather followers around him the nature of the journey is not nearly as clear as it had been for men like Moses or women like Ruth. Unlike their Old Testament forebears, these people can be told nothing about their destination, since it is not clear. Maybe this is why Jesus is at great pains to dissuade those who would follow him unthinkingly. When a member of the crowd steps forward with a pledge to follow Jesus wherever he may go, Jesus warns him that the road ahead may be far from comfortable: 'Foxes have dens and birds have nests, but the Son of Man has nowhere to lay his head' (Luke 9:58). Equally, those who wish to follow him while keeping at least half an eye on things at home are told in no uncertain terms that such a half-hearted departure will not do: 'No one who puts a hand to the plough and looks back is fit for service in the kingdom of God' (Luke 9:62).

What we see here is not a Christ who does not *want* followers, but rather a Christ who wants them *with their eyes wide open*. He outlines the same principle a few chapters later where he warns about embarking naively on the journey with him. He points out that this is every bit as dangerous as starting to build a tower without checking your raw materials first, or embarking on a military campaign without a large enough army. The result is likely to be catastrophic either way. In the same passage he warns that: 'If anyone comes to me and does not hate father and mother, wife and children, brothers and sisters – yes, even their own life – such a person cannot be my disciple' (Luke 14:26). Even if we allow for some degree of Jewish hyperbole with the use of the word 'hate' here, this is still a very strong statement. We cannot embark upon a journey of any kind without leaving something or somebody behind.

On occasion, we have to experience a degree of hatred, or at least dissatisfaction, before it becomes possible to leave familiar things and places behind. As a pastor I see it as my duty to invest wholeheartedly in the church where I serve. Having said that, I have experienced on leaving every pastorate that there comes a point where the strong cords of love must loosen in order to make departure psychologically and emotionally possible.

The truth of Christ's warning would be played out by the disciples who left their boats behind to become 'fishers of men'. It would be proven too by Saul who abandoned the power and influence of the Sanhedrin to preach 'The Way'. At different times he would find himself rescued from an angry crowd by Roman soldiers, defending himself before a king and a governor, as well as enduring numerous imprisonments. Writing to the church at Corinth, he listed the costs of his journey since leaving the security of his place in the Jewish establishment. The list included beatings, shipwrecks, floggings and imprisonments (2 Corinthians 11:23–26). Sitting, chained, in a prison cell, or struggling up on to a beach from yet another shipwreck, Paul can have been in no doubt that he had left all the safety and security of his former life behind. Like Dorothy in *The Wizard of Oz* he was 'not in Kansas any more'.

Since then this insight has been lived out by every missionary who has ever left familiar shores and faces to preach the gospel. Home, with its familiar patterns, routines and rhythms, must be left behind if we are to embrace new horizons. Over the years, missions training has improved enormously in terms of helping potential missionaries to know what to expect. Missions syllabi include modules on culture shock, cultural sensitivity, and even reverse culture shock when returning for home assignments.

Furthermore, many missionaries will be encouraged to think seriously about 'cutting the umbilical cord' which links them to home just one click or one phone call away. This has become a far more pressing issue with the advance of technology. It is easier than it ever was to stay in touch with home, but harder than it ever was to leave its gravitational pull behind. With or without technological connection, each missionary must face seriously the costly impact of disengaging from home in order to engage elsewhere.

For the new believer, home was once a place where they lived in a kind of glorious spiritual isolation. In that place, Jesus was locked outside the front door, if he was anywhere to be seen. Meanwhile, on the inside they could eat what they liked, drink what they liked, do whatever they liked, and indulge every whim or vice which took their fancy. When the front door is unlocked, and the command to 'follow me' is heeded, everything changes.

I sometimes fear that we have underplayed this aspect of conversion in our preaching of the gospel. Our language has become the sales pitch of the holiday brochure rather than the cautionary tale of the travel agent. We have been so keen to emphasize the distant and final shore to which the Christian is heading that we have underplayed the realities of the journey, and the necessity of leaving anything behind. The invitation has been more 'Come to this place' than 'Leave that place'. As a sales pitch it is entirely understandable. However, it can have consequences later when people realize that they have severed their ties with old habits, places and preferences without ever expecting to do so. An ancient pilgrim, turning to look back over his shoulder at the receding roofs of the village, knew that the steps he was taking were grave ones.

Bracing for the Impact of Departure

When leaving home for any considerable length of time, we
need to think not just about those things which must be done
before we leave, but those things which we shall miss while
we are away. A change may indeed be 'as good as a rest' but all
change is perceived as loss somewhere along the line. To leave
home long term is to accept that many things will be different:

- **Food.** One of the hardest adjustments for many when
  travelling or staying long term abroad is to adjust to a new
  diet. The way things are cooked, how they are flavoured,
  how long they are cooked for and even what is thought
  to be edible may all be very different. Sometimes even
  the familiar things seem strange. On a visit to Pakistan
  I remember being very surprised the first time I was served
  red carrots.
- **Drink.** 'Can I drink the water?' is a cliché of exotic travel,
  but this most staple of elements can be a real challenge in re-
  mote places. Travellers who fill a glass at the tap several times
  a day at home often find themselves on a quest for bottled
  water with a clearly unbroken seal before they are prepared
  to drink it.
- **Habits.** We like to think that fundamentally all human beings are the same. While that concept might be philosoph-
  ically true, there are many things which may challenge it
  when travelling away from home. Everything from how we
  greet each other to toiletry habits and humour may be vastly
  different from one place to another. In some countries people never queue, while in others they form an orderly line
  for the least excuse. In some they park their cars neatly in
  rows, while in others they seem to just stop and pull out

the key wherever the whim takes them. People who find the whole business of tipping in a restaurant difficult at home will struggle even more abroad.

- **Language.** The old-fashioned phrase book may well be giving way to the translation app on a smartphone, but either way it will not be long when travelling abroad before you become painfully aware that these people don't speak like you do. Sometimes this is at its most acute when people come from countries which share the same language but speak it differently. I remember describing a delicate pastoral situation to an Australian colleague, who described it as 'so ordinary'. I was momentarily offended, until he explained that for him it meant something which was trying or difficult.

- **Music.** You don't have to be an enthusiastic music fan to realize that there are significant differences in the music we hear in different cultures. Everything from the choice of instruments to the beat and tempo may be radically different, and these things will intrude on your hearing even if you are not consciously 'listening out' for the music. Oddly, there are some melodies which surface in various cultures around the world with no apparent explanation for how they got there. Even so, a familiar melody played with an unfamiliar tempo can be barely recognizable.

- **Time.** Travel too far from home and you are almost certain to have to adjust your watch. If you go far enough, people at home may be just going to bed as you get up, or out partying just as you lay your head on the pillow. After a while, this can make it hard even to picture people back home when you are away from them.

The prudent traveller takes all these things into consideration when they leave home. Maybe they find themselves a little quiet space to reflect on all that has been, before the taxi comes. Maybe they choose to arrive at the railway station or airport a couple of hours early specifically so as to process these things in their minds. With pilgrimage becoming big business in mainland Europe once again, the Pilgrim Office in Santiago de Compostela offers all manner of guidance to would-be pilgrims, including advice to think such things through. The *Guía Espiritual* issued by the Pilgrim Office asks would-be pilgrims to consider some of this: 'What has led you to undertake the Camino? What are you endeavouring to obtain or reach? On the Camino de Santiago you will experience sun, rain, tired feet and joy, but also thirst, hunger and adverse situations. You will ask yourself whether it was worth embarking on.'[3]

It is good to know that modern-day pilgrims may get more advice when they leave home than their forebears of centuries gone by. What about the pilgrim on the journey of faith, though? Have we warned her, or him, that there will be things to leave behind in order to follow Jesus? Think about it: as a new believer so many things change. Our *diet* is different, finding that different things sustain us. Over time we may even find that, like Jesus, 'doing the will of the Father' becomes like meat and drink to us. Our *habits* begin to change as we absorb the essence of the Christian community. This is not a quick transformation, like a chameleon colouring up on a bright green leaf, but it does happen. Habits of prayer, Bible reading, stewardship, generosity and truth begin to take up residence in the heart.

Our *language* changes too. I am not talking about some awful sort of 'Christianese' where our speech is peppered with inexplicable 'thees' and 'thous'. Rather, over time, there is a kindness and gentleness which creeps into the language of the Christian. With years of grace, the tone of our speech softens, and elements such as gossip and swearing start to get dropped from our vocabulary. I can remember a young man coming to visit me at church. He only visited once, and was still a little shell-shocked at the change which came over him. A television series filmed in a monastery had led him to ask questions of a Christian colleague at work. One thing had led to another, and he ended up embracing the Christian faith for himself. With a puzzled expression he looked at me and said, 'I don't even want to swear any more.'

The background *music* to our lives changes too, as Christians are those who 'march to a different drum'. I am not suggesting that every new Christian clears out their music library, whether digital or physical, and replaces it with Christian worship songs. Nonetheless, the melody of the heart is different. The tone of heaven becomes the fundamental frequency of the new creature in Christ, and the syncopated rhythm of Spirit and word becomes a familiar sound.

Finally, we find ourselves adapting to a different *time zone*. Of course our hours and minutes are the same as everybody else's – it's just that we count them differently. The minutes may tick by at the same pace they always did, but now we know they are not the sum total of what we have. All these things apply when the new Christian leaves their erstwhile 'home' to follow Jesus.

Formal rites of passage such as baptism and confirmation may imply the cost of departure, but we should surely make sure that it is fully understood beyond the rituals themselves. In a Baptist church a baptismal candidate is asked whether they will 'serve Christ in the church and follow him in the world wherever he may lead'. Confirmation candidates, meanwhile, declare that they will 'fight valiantly as a disciple of Christ against sin, the world and the devil, and remain faithful to

Christ to the end of your life'. In some branches of the church, particularly in parts of Africa, an adult who is baptized into the faith may change their name from that moment onwards – a powerful reminder that home has been left behind.

An explanation of the cost of 'leaving home' should perhaps be part of the preaching of the gospel, rather than a follow-up to it. We should describe these costs as 'part of the deal', rather than allowing people to find out for themselves at a later stage, with all the risks that entails. The medieval pilgrim, standing on the edge of his village waving goodbye to family and friends, his farm entrusted to another and his oath sworn to the priest, could have had no doubts about the gravity of his move. The modern disciple may not be quite so clear.

Making a Good Departure

Since we all love to dream about changing our lives completely, there is a rich vein of television programmes on the theme of 'living the dream', or similar. One of them always featured people making drastic moves – uprooting their entire lives from one side, or one end, of the world to the other. Much of the programme would be taken up with the practicalities of finding a job, selecting a house, organizing schooling, and other vital elements. Always, though, towards the end of the programme there would be a party thrown for friends and neighbours before leaving home for good. Nine times out of ten the camera would pull discreetly away from the lighted windows to the sound of tears mixed with the clinking of glasses and laughter. It happened so often it was almost a cliché, but it was making a valid point about the need for a good departure. The implication was often there that it was only at this moment, with family and friends from whom they were about to be parted all around them, that the full cost of 'living the dream' came home to roost.

We try to make good departures in other ways too. When people leave their job to take up another, the office whip-round for a small gift and a 'do' to send them off are seen as inevitable. When people retire, we would think it odd if their employer did not mark it with some kind of presentation in front of their colleagues. These things are a recognition of the rhythms at the heart of human life. When we wrench ourselves out of one pattern and insert ourselves into another, we do not do so lightly. The body, mind and emotions reel with a shock which is almost physical in its intensity. For every person who dreams wistfully of a peaceful retirement while looking out of the office window, there is another who gazes wistfully at the bus-stop queue through the kitchen window and wishes they still needed to be on it. Pre-retirement courses, leaving dos and send-offs of every kind are a recognition of this. Isn't it time we recognized the enormous impact of the wrench we experience when we embark on the disciple's journey of faith?

Many pilgrims in earlier centuries would leave home after a blessing from the parish priest and a service of departure with the local bishop. Those walking the Camino from France on into Spain would stop at the monastery of Roncesvalles, not far into their long journey. The evening mass would include the following prayer:

Oh God, You who took up your servant Abraham from the city of Ur of the Chaldeans, watching over him in all his wanderings.

You who were the guide of the Hebrew people in the desert, we ask that You deign to take care of these your servants who, for love of Your name, make a pilgrimage to Compostela.

Be a companion for them along the path, a guide at crossroads, strength in their weariness, defense before dangers, shelter on the way, shade against the heat, light in the darkness, a comforter in their discouragements, and firmness in their intentions, in order that, through your guidance, they might arrive unscathed at the end of their journey and, enriched with graces and virtues, they might return safely to their homes, which now lament their absence, filled with salutary and lasting joy.

Through Jesus Christ Your Son, Who lives and reigns with You, in the unity of the Holy Spirit, one God, for ever and ever.

May the blessing of Almighty God, Father, Son and Holy Spirit, descend on you.[4]

Hearing such words, they could be left in no doubt that home really was left behind them, and that the journey, with all its challenges, lay ahead. This was a serious and solemn departure, but one wreathed in prayer and reflection.

If you happen to be at a major railway station or busy airport you will be unable to avoid hearing people say goodbye. In fact, that is not entirely true. You will hear many say 'See you', or blow a kiss, or even use the shortened form 'Bye', but 'Goodbye' has gone out of fashion. The origins of the word were a plea that God go 'by' or with you. In an age where many journeys were beset with perils of every kind, the wish made perfect sense. I sometimes wish that the word were still in common currency. After all, what better words could we say to a person setting out on the journey of their lives than these? 'Goodbye' is at once a recognition of the departure's enormity and a reassurance that God, who was at its start, will be present both in its duration and its end.

For Reflection

1. We often like to emphasize that Christianity is *not* a list of 'thou shalt *not*' instructions. If you were advising a new Christian, or an enquirer, what would you say they *did* have to leave behind in order to embark on the journey of faith?
2. Thinking back to the start of your Christian journey, what are the things which you found hardest to leave behind?
3. Think back to some of the characters mentioned earlier in this chapter – Moses, Abram, Naomi and Ruth. If you were raising a glass at their leaving party before the journey began, what would you say in the toast?
4. Look back at the pilgrims' prayer from Roncesvalles, quoted earlier in this chapter. If you had to write a prayer for a disciple setting out on the journey of faith, what would you write? You may find this exercise easier if you can insert the name of a particular person.

Provisions by Max Ellis

3

Provisions

In 2003 Jack Hitt, a *New York Times* journalist, took the decision to walk the Camino de Santiago. He was not a Christian pilgrim. In fact, he would not even describe himself as a Christian, but all the same the lure of that particular open road proved too much to resist. Maps studied, plane tickets booked and schedule cleared, he headed to the local outdoor and camping shop to buy what he thought would be a few accessories to help with the journey. He came away with everything from lycra boots and specialized socks to hurricane-proof tents and sleeping bags. If the modern-day pilgrim were to travel light at all, it would only be because the high-tech materials of which his equipment was fashioned weighed little.

Hitt's medieval forebears would have stared in wonder at his mound of equipment, and probably shaken their heads at such excess. The traditional pilgrim's equipment was simple, lightweight and unpretentious. It would have consisted of the following:

- **A floppy hat** – to protect him from the sun and the worst of the rain
- **A cloak** – which would provide warmth on early mornings and late nights, and could be wrapped around to provide a rudimentary tent should the need arise

- **A staff** – this would provide the pilgrim with something on which to lean when weary, and a means to beat down the undergrowth should the path be overgrown
- **A scrip** – a small bag no bigger than a modern 'bum bag', which would have had room for little more than one day's ration of food
- **A gourd** – a hollowed-out gourd would provide a simple means to carry and drink water
- **Sandals** – few pilgrims could afford closed-in boots, but would wear the best footwear they could find
- **A token** – pilgrims would often wear a token associated with their particular pilgrimage. In the instance of the Camino de Santiago, this would be a scallop shell, in honour of St James. Early pilgrims to Winchester wore them too, and we shall read the tale of a very special shell token in Chapter 12.

The lines below are from a seventeenth-century poem entitled 'The Passionate Man's Pilgrimage'. Originally accredited to Sir Walter Raleigh, the source has since been called into question.

> Give me my scallop-shell of quiet,
> My staff of faith to walk upon,
> My scrip of joy, immortal diet,
> My bottle of salvation,
> My gown of glory, hope's true gage;
> And thus I'll take my pilgrimage.[1]

What is significant, though, is that the list of pilgrim's equipment mirrors so perfectly the list above. Whoever wrote it, both writer and readers would clearly recognize a pilgrim when they saw one.

Each item of the pilgrim's equipment fulfilled a particular function, from protection to provision. However, between them they served another purpose. This pilgrim's 'uniform' served to protect the pilgrim on his way through many countries and across many borders. With his cloak about his shoulders and his scrip at his waist, the pilgrim could not fall prey to the national law of each country through which he passed. Instead, he fell under the jurisdiction of a 'pilgrim's code', which was effectively the forerunner of international law. The pilgrim's possessions were few, but they served to protect, provide and sustain him throughout the journey. To this day, some of this tradition continues, with a blessing of rucksack and staff offered at Roncesvalles monastery early along the Camino route:

> In the name of our Lord Jesus Christ, receive this pouch, habit for your pilgrimage, so that, castigated and corrected, you hasten to prostrate at Saint James' feet, where you yearn to arrive and, after having completed your journey, you come to us delighted with the help of God, who rules over the world without end. Amen.

> Receive this staff as support for the journey and your efforts during your pilgrimage so that you are able to defeat the throngs of enemies and thus arrive safely at Saint James' feet and, after having completed your journey, you come to us delighted with the consent of the same God, who lives in and rules over Heaven without end. Amen.

> In the name of the Lord Jesus Christ, shoulder these rucksacks which will help you during your pilgrimage. May the fatigue of carrying them be expiation for your sins, so that when you have been forgiven you may reach the shrine of St James full of courage, and when your pilgrimage is over, return home full of joy. We ask this through Christ our Lord.[2]

The pilgrim's possessions, few though they be, become precious companions along the way. At those moments of the journey when no one else is there to share the reflections or comment upon the passing landscape, the comfort of a strong staff or a windproof cloak may have been very great indeed. Those who wear a uniform in the police or armed forces will probably understand the uniform as an internal as well as external reference point. In other words, the soldier who dons a uniform not only looks like a soldier; he or she *feels* like one too. The pilgrims' garb, and their few possessions, marks them out to others along the way, but also serves as a reminder to each who wears it of the home they have left behind and the journey upon which they have embarked.

Travelling Light

As we have already seen, there is a rich vein of journey running all the way through Scripture. From Adam leaving the shelter of Eden, and Noah embarking upon his gargantuan boat, to fisherman Peter following his Lord, or Paul moving relentlessly towards Rome, the journey is ever present. Something else we notice, though, is that the journey is often travelled light.

Moses and the exodus

When Moses left the palace one morning and ended up falling into an argument with a slave-driver, it was a journey from which he would never return. The argument turned into some kind of rage, he struck the slave-driver dead, and he fled immediately into Midian as a wanted fugitive. It is highly unlikely that he ever returned to the palace, and so we must assume he travelled only with what he wore. Years later, God called him back from obscurity and he returned to Egypt to face down the pharaoh and demand the people's freedom. As the plagues became more and more terrible, the night came for the hardest showdown of all: the Passover. Detailed instructions were given on what was to be eaten, and the people were even told how to eat their meal: 'When you eat the meal, be dressed and ready to travel. Have your sandals on, carry your walking stick in your hand, and eat quickly. This is the Passover Festival in honour of me, your LORD' (Exodus 12:11 CEV).

If I remember correctly, my mother would have had something to say about eating your meal standing up and dressed to go out of the door! This seems designed to induce discomfort, to say nothing of indigestion, in the eaters. However, it served as a reminder to the Hebrews that this was the start of a journey where progress was more important than ease and they could carry only a limited amount with them. Ahead of them lay forty years of travelling, so they might as well start as they meant to go on. For a whole generation, their lives would be temporary ones. Their homes would be tents which could be packed away at a moment's notice, and their possessions would be only those things which they could carry on a journey of indeterminate length.

It is tempting to feel that the Bible devotes inordinate amounts of space to the descriptions of the tabernacle. Overall it is mentioned in forty-eight different chapters of the Old Testament and two of the New. Every detail is covered, from the metalwork designs on the finials which would hold the tent up, to the woven designs on the different coverings, and even the way in which the poles to carry it all should be fashioned. All this serves to underline that the people were not the only ones on the move. God was coming with them, and his presence would be represented by this 'folding temple' whose design meant that they could carry it with them across all the miles which lay ahead.

Of course, even if they could carry the temple with them, there was no way they could carry enough food for such a journey. Not only that, but there was no way they could linger long enough to grow crops. A few months into the journey all their livestock would have been slaughtered and they found themselves in an inhospitable landscape. God alone could provide their food and drink, with manna from heaven and water from the rock. Interestingly, it is the water gushing from the rock which is the single most common Old Testament image to be found in the catacombs of Rome. Centuries after the exodus, with God's people again forced to live like strangers in the world, there was comfort to be found in this reminder that God would provide.

Elijah and the ravens

Years after Moses, with the exodus little more than a folk memory, the great prophet Elijah was a thorn in the sides of King Ahab and Queen Jezebel. Eventually things came to a head on Mount Carmel between Elijah and the prophets of Baal. Many died that day, and Queen Jezebel was out for his blood. With no time to head home, he ran and ran for his life. He ended up in a desert wadi with a small stream running through it. How was he to survive? On what was this religious fugitive to dine? Once more, God had to provide miraculously. Every morning and every evening, ravens would swoop in over the horizon, bearing food for him to eat. Elijah could neither stockpile nor plan, but had to look to the sky, and to God, for his daily rations: 'Leave here, turn eastward and hide in the Kerith Ravine, east of the Jordan. You will drink from the brook, and I have instructed the ravens to supply you with food there' (1 Kings 17:3–4).

Maybe these were the same lessons he employed when he reassured the widow at Zarephath, with such certainty, that she need have no fear in using her last resources to make him a meal. God would provide for her, and her son, for many days to come (see 1 Kings 17:7–16). Sometimes these lessons learned 'on the road', when the sun beats down and the way seems long, can be applied in the small 'domestic' space of another time and another crisis.

Gideon and his shrinking army

Gideon appears in Scripture at a difficult moment in the history of God's people. Cross-border raids from their warlike neighbours are commonplace, and we first meet Gideon threshing corn inside a wine vat – an occupation which is as ridiculous as it is desperate. Small wonder that he was taken aback by the angel's greeting: 'The LORD is with you, mighty warrior' (Judges 6:12).

Once he has recovered from the shock of his angelic visitation, and reassured himself in numerous ways that the angel's message is genuine, Gideon accepts his calling. Despite being the weakest member of the smallest family of one of the lesser tribes, he is to be the man to defeat his people's enemies. He sets out to find himself an army and issues a call to arms. Thirty-two thousand men respond, but God is not happy. He tells Gideon to reduce the size of the army, and he issues a

decree that anyone who is afraid of the fight may return home –
an offer which 22,000 accept. God is still not happy, though.
He sets them a test to see who keeps their guard while drinking
water, and who drops it. Nine thousand, seven hundred men
fail the test, and Gideon is left with an army of only 300 with
which to defeat his enemies. Throughout this process, Gideon
is undergoing a deliberate diminution of his resources in order
to maximize his reliance upon God.

Twelve disciples, seventy-two missionaries and not a support vehicle between them

Many centuries later, and Jesus is commissioning his disciples
to go out and spread the word in the towns and villages of their
region. They might have expected a motivational speech, of the
'eve of battle' variety, which they certainly got. However, many
would have been dismayed at their kit list. Given that many of
these men would never have left their own village before, the
journey ahead was a daunting one. A little home comfort here
or there would not have gone amiss, surely? Jesus, however, instructs them that they are to travel light and avoid distraction:
'Do not take a purse or bag or sandals; and do not greet anyone
on the road' (Luke 10:4).

Like their Old Testament forebears, crossing deserts and
mountains, they were not to weigh themselves down with spare
clothing or footwear. Instead, the one who called them would
ensure that their needs were met. Before the time when they set
out truly on their own, they would see ample evidence of God's
ability and inclination to provide. Jesus himself, who began
his life in a borrowed womb and a borrowed bed, would show
them how it was done. In a similar way he told enthusiastic

aspiring disciples that they should not expect either comfort or ease. They would be provided for, but only as they exercised faith, and only insofar as they needed it. 'Foxes have dens and birds have nests, but the Son of Man has nowhere to lay his head' (Luke 9:58).

The rich man and his needle

When Jesus began to teach in public, it was not just his miracles, but also his words, which caused a stir. Great crowds, with everyone from religious devotees to intrigued passers-by, would stop to listen to him. For some it was the stories which drew them in, while others were captivated by a tone of real religious authority which they had not heard elsewhere. When a devout young man stood before Jesus and told him that he had led an exemplary life, he seemed to get short shrift from the Teacher, telling him to 'go, sell everything you have and give to the poor, and you will have treasure in heaven' (Mark 10:21). This was not a demand Jesus made of anybody else, let alone a person who had made such spiritual strides. Why the harsh treatment? For each person, the bond which anchors them to a safe place other than God's kingdom is different. For him, it was his wealth, and without letting go of it he could not leave home and join God's pilgrim people.

Paul and his needle

Paul was the most influential of the church's early missionaries. He took the gospel and carried it beyond the household of Israel to the shores of Europe. Churches in Turkey, Italy,

Macedonia and other European countries can speak of their Pauline heritage. There are no blue plaques, though, to say that 'Paul lived here'. There are not even any ruins of where the great man's house might have stood. The fact is, he was an itinerant preacher from beginning to end, with no permanent base. From the moment when he stumbled, blind, into Simon the Tanner's house on Straight Street in Damascus, we are not aware that he ever had a place to call his own. Not only that, but all those arrows in the backs of Bibles which depict his missionary journeys depict self-financed travel. In order to avoid placing a financial burden upon his hosts, and maybe to void any whiff of 'patronage', Paul 'worked his way' through the missionary journeys. Like a modern-day gap-year student on a round-the-world ticket, he moved from job to job and town to town. There is an irony that the European church, so reliant upon his itinerant and impoverished missionary work, is now among the most deeply rooted and established pillars of society.

Moses, Elijah, Gideon, Paul and others all learned to travel lean and light. The writer to the Hebrews talks about God's people as those who 'did not receive the things promised; they only saw them and welcomed them from a distance' (Hebrews 11:13). He went on to describe them as those who were 'longing for a better country' (Hebrews 11:16). Travelling light, un-comforted by permanent homes and unencumbered by luxurious possessions, God's people are constantly on the move, living on the rations carried or provided along the way. Maybe this is why part of the promise contained in the book of Revelation is that no one will go hungry or thirsty again. Those who live their lives on the road are used to a lean diet, since everything which is to be consumed must also be carried.

God Will Provide

For many years I have been a fan of Bill Bryson's writing. His warm self-deprecating humour and his observational wit are a joy to read. Many of his books have been known to make me laugh out loud in trains, in bed, and in an occasional hospital waiting room. *A Walk in the Woods* is different, though. In it, he tells the story of the attempt made by him and his lifelong friend, Katz, to walk the Appalachian Trail. There is real pathos in the book, as the two of them encounter the darker side of the wild country the trail crosses. At the outset, on the first morning of their journey, they set out from their hotel full of anticipation. Katz, however, has brought far too much with him. By the time he has crested the first hill, he has jettisoned all manner of food and equipment from his rucksack in order to make the journey possible. He had failed to pack light, and lived to regret it. Young people training for their Duke of Edinburgh award often find the same thing. I know one young man who packed his rucksack two thirds full with tins of baked beans and sausage – on the grounds that they would be comforting to eat when he got the opportunity. Sadly, he was so exhausted from carrying them around that he barely had the energy to eat them, let alone heat them.

For the early pilgrims, the obligation to travel with minimal possessions was not only a practical, but a spiritual requirement. To travel light, not to know where the next meal or the next bed was to be found, was to link them in an unbroken thread to the heroes of Old and New Testament who had gone before them. In their village churches they had heard the tales of these men and women told over and over again since their childhood. Now was the time to start experiencing those tales for themselves. These were lessons not only for the travellers, but also for those who would take them in. The onward march of the early church had been reliant on hospitality and generous provision to fuel it. This is why John thanks the recipients of his third letter for their legendary hospitality and for sending the saints on their way in 'a manner worthy of God' (3 John 6 esv).

When I was in the early stages of writing this book, I bumped into a friend who had participated in the UK 'Walk of 1,000 Men' some years ago. This was a men's evangelistic crusade, designed to engage many men in the business of spreading the gospel in Britain's villages. In teams of ten they set out, with no money or provisions, to see where the journey would take them. My friend had tale after tale to tell of his experience of miraculous provisions. On one occasion, he woke his team in a chilly church hall, and decided to stave off the hunger pangs by praying. Their prayers were interrupted by a soft knock on the door. Tentatively, a villager poked her head around the door to say that if the men made their way to the end of the village, they would find that the café had opened early just for them, to provide them with a free breakfast. They ate well, and left the village with a spring in their step. The story was to be repeated again and again.

Often we have to go without our familiar comfort and provision in order to grow our faith. In this sense, growing our faith is like growing our muscles. We need to stretch them a little more each time in order to increase our capacity. In fact, muscles grow when tiny fibres are torn through exertion; muscle fibre then grows to take on the gap, and so on. Our muscles hurt when they grow, as fibres separate again and again. The summer when this book was first born was the summer when I attempted the greatest physical feat I have ever undertaken. As a child I used to 'mess about' on a bike, as most kids do. Since then, I had used it only occasionally. However, when I saw an invitation to undertake a charity cycle ride for a beloved local hospice, I agreed to the challenge. Starting in February I began to ride first 10, then 20, then 40 kilometres at a time. Six days before the event I did my biggest training ride – 72 km. When the night came, I knew that the full 100 km was within my reach. It was hard work, and I ached the next day, but the night of 8 June 2013 saw me riding the full 100 km around London, past some of its greatest landmarks and up some of its steepest hills. The only way to know whether or not I was capable of it was to try.

For many pilgrims both old and new, raised on a spiritual diet of sermons about God's provision, the only way to see whether they could follow in those illustrious footsteps was to try it for themselves. The trouble is, the greater the number of our possessions, the harder it is for us to contemplate life without them. Sometimes people talk about *affluenza* or 'acquisitiveness' as a peculiarly modern affliction for the believer, but I am unconvinced. It seems to me that as long as we have had possessions we have also had difficulty holding onto them lightly. The oldest saying attributed to Jesus to be found anywhere in the world outside the Bible is carved in Arabic at a palace in Fatehpur Sikri, Uttar Pradesh. Above a gateway to the old palace it says: 'The world is a bridge; pass over it, but build no houses upon it.' Writing in similar vein in the fourth century, St John Chrysostom wrote, 'I beg you therefore, while we are pilgrims in this world and soldiers on earth, let us not build for ourselves houses to settle down in but make tents we can leave at a moment's notice.'[3] This is easier said than done for those who have established lives with houses and possessions and all the trappings which accompany them. All is not lost, though.

Triage

When I was a teenager, my first real encounter with overseas mission work came when my two beloved youth leaders, Chris and Janet, answered a call to serve overseas as missionaries in Swaziland. With such generous hearts, they allowed a bunch of awkward teenagers to help them with their preparations for the big adventure. I can trace my own interest in overseas mission to the afternoon I spent in Chris and Janet's house sorting books into 'ditch' and 'keep' piles, and then packing the latter into crates ready for shipping. From that moment on, mission became personal.

Many overseas missionaries who have trodden the same path as my dear friends have been through a cathartic experience in relation to their possessions. The strength of their call to serve elsewhere outweighs the bond they thought they had to so many of their possessions. Once upon a time they might have seemed precious, but in the light of a greater calling they take on another perspective. Some friends who spent over twenty years serving in Ethiopia were there through some of the worst months of the civil war. When the fighting reached its most intense and they were ordered to evacuate their home, they were given just five minutes to collect any belongings. They looked around at all the things they had acquired and concluded that the only possession precious enough to save was the list of students for whom they regularly prayed. Such situations are a drastic way to sever our chronic acquisitiveness, but the liberation can be immense.

Kosuke Koyama, whom we first met in Chapter 1, was a Japanese citizen who later became a professor of theology in Union Theological Seminary. He was a great advocate for simplicity, stating that Christians had 'no limousines' and warning that a self-interested Christianity would turn into an 'ugly monster'.[4] His book, *Three Mile an Hour God*, was a great influence on me in the early stages of researching this one. Maybe one of the magnets which draws people into pilgrimage, from every faith and none, is the desire to break the bonds which possessions hold over those who possess them. The pilgrim who starts off missing the things he or she leaves behind may end up feeling no great compulsion to ever take them up again. Nancy Louise Frey comments that 'the desire to go lightly in life becomes translated to the Camino through the backpack'.[5] This may be one of the reasons that there were towns close to the end of the Camino de Santiago which became effectively French colonies. The people who had trekked so far from home in northern France felt disinclined to return to their lives as they had left them. We look at this later on in Chapter 8.

Sometimes we smirk at the festival-goer who still wears their summer wristband in the cold months of winter, or the ex-pilgrim who still carries the badge stitched onto their coat or fixed to their walking stick. Maybe, though, they are trying to remind themselves in the humdrum of everyday life that things can be simpler if we want them to be. Of course, a physical symbol is not necessary in order to remember that. Pilgrims arriving at the end of their pilgrimage in the English city of Winchester would sometimes toss their scallop-shell emblems into the river at the end of their journey. To do so was a dramatic gesture of thanks to the saint for protection on their journey, but also a reminder that the pilgrimage was over and they would now have to return to ordinary things. Keeping the trappings of the journey, a bit like God's people keeping leftover manna, can blind us to the provision which comes tomorrow by our focus on that which came yesterday . . .

For Reflection

1. We all like to think that we are *not* tied to our possessions, and that the old adage about 'love people and use things' applies to us. If you were to make an inventory of those things which you feel you could not do without, what would come nearest to the top of the list?
2. Was it 'unfair' of Jesus to ask the rich young man to go without his possessions? If you had been there, how might you have explained it afterwards to the young man himself?
3. Out of all the stories of 'travelling light' we have read in this chapter, which one means the most to you, and why?
4. Each pilgrimage carried a particular symbol, or 'badge'. What symbol would best describe your journey to date?

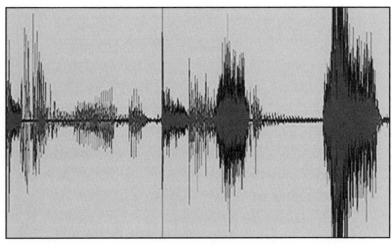

Communications by the voice of Richard Littledale

4

Communications

A few years ago, I was on holiday in the spectacular Jura, just on the borders of France and Switzerland. In summer it is a land of still waters, sweeping mountains and alpine pastures. On one occasion, we went to visit a set of waterfalls which feeds one of the larger lakes. The falls have a visitor and interpretation centre, where visitors pay their money and pick up a trail leaflet to guide them through the steep forest paths. No sooner has the visitor left the centre than they encounter a warning sign in multiple languages accompanied by pictograms. It warns visitors that there are parts of the path through the forest where it will not be possible to have a mobile signal. For many in an 'always on' culture, this is a profoundly unsettling prospect. After all, distance is usually no object – with people skyping from the International Space Station or tweeting from the Space Shuttle. When something as simple and ancient as a mountain path gets in our way and blocks up our communication channels, we can experience a kind of acute separation anxiety.

These days, people in orbiting spacecraft, roaring Formula 1 cars or flimsy round-the-world sailing boats have every expectation of staying in touch with the support team at home throughout their journey. When yachtswoman Ellen MacArthur completed her solo yacht journey of 25,354 miles around the world, she paid tribute to all those who had stayed in touch with her throughout the seventy-one days of the journey. 'When I was out there I was never ever alone; there was always a team of people behind me, in mind if not in body.'[1]

Some friends of mine recently completed a new pilgrimage route in the UK, and they described it as a 'digital' pilgrimage – staying in touch with friends and supporters by text, tweet, Instagram and audio/video blog all the way round. On the positive side, this allowed many others to share in their experience of pilgrimage, even from other parts of the country or other countries. On the other hand, it deprived them of the very isolation which could be seen as essential to the act of pilgrimage.

Some colleagues who worked in an international mission agency found that modern email communication was a distinctly mixed blessing. They described it as being too much of an 'umbilical cord' between the missionary overseas and their supporters at home. In the days when a letter could take two weeks to get home, and another two weeks for a reply to come back, missionaries learned to adapt more quickly to their new environment, and make decisions for themselves without advice from home. Missions experts could, of course, argue this both ways. What is certain, however, is that people on any kind of 'spiritual adventure' expect to be able to stay in touch with those they have left behind. For the medieval pilgrim this would have been impossible. Many could not write, and even if they did, the prospect of a letter making it all the way home, across borders and oceans, was all but impossible.

For the pilgrim, with his or her familiar world shrinking in the distance, communications take on a new perspective. Conversations with old friends and beloved family become a thing of the past, to be replaced with other encounters. The pilgrim strikes up new conversations with travelling companions along the way and also finds conversation with God born out of the solitude.

Talking with God

We have seen already how the story of Scripture is shot through with the motif of journeying. Often these journeys are arduous, intimidating, and in some instances almost terrifying. Think of Abram, for instance, asked at the age of 75 to leave behind every familiar thing and go off to a land he had never seen. Moses, similarly, is asked to leave every familiar thing behind. After the splendour of the royal palace and the ignominy of his enforced exile, the prospect of leading God's people to freedom must have seemed preposterous at best. With the journey under way, things go from bad to worse when the people turn against Moses and create an idol to worship – a golden calf. The incident is dealt with, many die, and it is time to move on again. Moses, however, digs his heels in and says to God that he cannot travel alone: 'If your Presence does not go with us, do not send us up from here' (Exodus 33:15).

Many a pilgrim, with the priest's blessing still ringing in their ears as the hills of home fell away in the distance, must have said a similar thing. Their arduous journey would have been impossible without God and barely possible with him. Thus the pilgrim's route becomes a path of prayer, where conversations with God resound with every footfall.

Jonah, far from home and experiencing the worst kind of journey, learns to pray as never before. There is a searing honesty to his angry prayer from the belly of the whale, and to the clarion call of faith as he declares that he will worship God in daylight once again: 'What I have vowed I will make good' (Jonah 2:9).

Many pilgrims facing the loneliest parts of the journey and the worst of weather conditions have cried out to God as never before. Jack Hitt, a self-confessed atheist who nonetheless undertook the Camino de Santiago, confessed to praying in the midst of a violent and terrifying electrical storm in the Meseta plains. Out there, in an unfamiliar landscape, prayer didn't seem like such a strange thing after all. The rigours of the journey and the unforgiving landscape somehow made prayer seem both natural and acceptable to him. A little while ago I found myself on a live radio show with an unusual fellow guest. He is a TV and film stuntman who made his name by parachuting into the Olympic Stadium in 2012 dressed as the Queen. He now harbours ambitions to equal, or exceed, the longest freefall jump in history. The subject of fears came up, and he confessed that many professional jumpers who claim no religious allegiance have been known to pray on the way down. In a similar vein, it is sometimes claimed that there were no atheists in the trenches in the First World War. Even those who claim no religious affiliation of any kind will talk about 'praying' when the need is great enough. Extreme circumstances can make prayer seem like the most natural thing in the world.

When King David reflects on his years, he remembers that God heard him in the worst of times. By the time he wrote Psalm 55 he had been a shepherd boy, a court musician, a fugitive, a rebel fighter and a king. In all of that, he could remember no circumstance where God had not listened to him: 'Evening, morning and noon I cry out in distress, and he hears my voice' (Psalm 55:17).

In the undulating path of the pilgrim – up the hills, through the valleys, under the forest canopies and across the bare mountains – prayer can become just another rhythm. The tramp, tramp, tramp of the pilgrim's foot can become like a metronome for the voice of prayer. Those who designed medieval monasteries recognized the importance of this, which is why they included cloisters. These represented an almost indoor space where the outdoor journey of the pilgrim could be mimicked. Those wishing to talk to God to the background music of their footsteps could do so in the cloister without ever leaving the walls of the monastery.

I used to walk past a garden which bore (alongside a scattering of gnomes) a plaque with the following verse on it:

> The kiss of the sun for pardon
> The song of the birds for mirth,
> One is closer to God in a garden
> Than any place on earth.[2]

For me it was the worst kind of kitsch theology, not least because I am an awful gardener. If God were to be present in any garden, I suspect it might not be mine! In the strictest theological terms, we are no closer to God in any one place than any other place. Nowhere is especially holy, because everywhere is especially holy. A few years ago I decided to conduct some research on the subject of 'awe'. Where, exactly, did people experience it? I created an interactive online map, and invited people to push a pin into the place where they had experienced a feeling which they would describe as awe. To date, the results are as follows:

- 540+ views
- 43 map pins
- 24 pins are on sites of natural beauty
- 3 are in non-religious buildings

- 8 are in churches, both great and small
- 8 indicate that a sense of awe is drawn from human beings.

With the high proportion of pins placed in sites of natural beauty, we should maybe not be surprised that the walking pilgrim expects to meet God along the way. In researching this book I have been amazed by the number of those who set out to write a book which is no more than a spiritually neutral travelogue, and end up with something which touches upon a spiritual nerve. This applies not only to writers like Hitt and Stanford who set out to walk the pilgrim path, but to Solnit with her history of walking, and Cracknell with her account of ten walks remembered. It even crops up in Paul Smith's book *Twitchhiker*, where his journey around the world by Twitter brings him face to face with fundamental human goodness. He ends up by describing Twitter as 'a user-defined infrastructure that can be harnessed to change lives and expectations, to share and enhance unique experiences and viewpoints'.[3] You don't have to go out looking for a transcendent experience on the road, it would seem. That experience may well come looking for you.

Walking and Talking

On a recent package holiday to Italy, the journey from airport to hotel was accompanied by the usual patter from the holiday adviser. (Apparently the title 'rep' is no longer acceptable.) There was the predictable smattering of practical instructions, some recommendations on local food and wines, a sales pitch for excursions, and a couple of useful Italian phrases thrown in for good measure. What was different, though, was the offer of a 'radical' new meeting for new guests the next morning.

Instead of sipping cappuccinos in the lobby of a local hotel we would walk the streets, meeting local traders and seeing the area for ourselves. In this way we would get a much better 'feel' for it. The only surprising thing about this was that it was new. Of course the best way to make sense of a place is to walk around it with someone who has been there before and allow them to orientate you within it.

In her magnificent analysis of the history of walking, *Wanderlust*, Rebecca Solnit talks about walking as the finest way to make sense of the physical world which we inhabit. A landscape may be observed in its entirety from the air, or taken in through the windows of a speeding train or a driving car. However, to really make sense of it, it has to be walked. Solnit argues that walking makes sense not only of the space traversed, but also of the one who traverses it: 'Walking has been one of the constellations in the starry sky of human culture, a constellation whose three stars are the body, the imagination and the wide-open world, and though all three exist independently, it is the lines drawn between them – drawn by the act of walking for cultural purposes – that makes them a constellation.'[4] A pilgrim walking the way may find that the conversations held with God en route bring more clarity and focus than could ever have been attained in an act of stationary prayer. Solnit, again, describes pilgrimage as 'the quest in search of something, if only one's own transformation'.[5]

In 2004 Jon Anderson, of Cardiff University, published a paper on 'bimbling' as the best means of discovering the social, geographical and historical interpretation of a given landscape. To 'bimble', or walk without firm purpose, through a landscape with one of its long-time residents could lead to a far richer understanding of it than could be gained either through reading or through listening to the same person out of context. He states that 'conversations held whilst walking through a place have the potential to generate a collage of collaborative knowledge'.[6] Furthermore, as we all know, walking can jog not just the body but the memory. Walking through an old school playing-field or the street where we used to live may generate all kinds of recollections about those places which would otherwise have eluded us. Anderson goes on to say that walking while talking can 'successfully tap into the non-mechanistic framework of the mind and its interconnections with place to recall episodes and meanings buried in the archaeology of knowledge'.[7] In other words, the movement of our feet may liberate both the flow of thought and the words with which to articulate it. Anyone who has ever walked vigorously while trying to untangle a knotty problem, or sauntered slowly while trying to find an elusive answer, will know what this is all about. Professor Robert Macfarlane, in his book *The Old Ways*, talks about 'walking as enabling sight and thought'.[8] In her history of walking, *Wanderlust*, Rebecca Solnit says that: 'Walking itself is the intentional act closest to the unwilled rhythms of the body, to breathing and the beating of the heart. It strikes a delicate balance between working and idling, being and doing. It is bodily labour that produces nothing but thoughts, experiences and arrivals.'[9]

There is a story told by American life coach Wayne Muller which recounts the habit of an (un-named) South American tribe whose members will walk fast for several days before stopping and making camp for a day or two before pressing on with the journey. Challenged about their reasons for doing this, one of the tribal leaders told a visitor that they were 'allowing their souls to catch up with them'.[10] The story is very popular with bloggers who write for busy audiences about the need to take time off. For some, though, it is not a change of activity but a change of pace which is needed.

American corporate culture, especially at the creative end of the spectrum, has enthusiastically endorsed the idea of the 'walking meeting'. Those arriving for an interview in the higher echelons of Silicon Valley may well find that it is conducted on the move. In 2014 psychologists Marily Oppezzo and Daniel Schwartz of Stanford University started putting this to the test. They noticed an increase in creative output of between 80 and 100 per cent when their test subjects were walking rather than sitting: 'Walking substantially enhanced creativity by two different measures.'[11] They concluded that 'many people anecdotally claim they do their best thinking when walking. We finally may be taking a step, or two, toward discovering why.'[12] Walking may allow us to untangle a problem, pace out a thought, or even to tread down a path which leads to God.

For the Christian it may do all of those things, and also enable prayer. It may enable us to both think of God and speak to God with a renewed liberty. Robert Mullen, in his book *The Call of the Camino*, describes meeting an artist who was sketching as she travelled the route. She drew a picture of a lone pilgrim walking the route towards a hilltop village where a bell tower could be seen in the distance. Underneath was a caption which said that 'to walk the Camino is to pray with one's feet'.[13] Where a Christian's prayer life has become stultified or frustrated, praying while walking may be just the injection of dynamic energy which it requires.

Walking and Praying

The link between spiritual communication and locomotion may go back some four thousand years to the earliest known labyrinths, whose precise purpose is lost to us. However, from what we know about thinking and walking we should not be surprised if they were regarded as an aid to some kind of communication with the divine. The earliest Christian example is to be found in the fourth-century Basilica of St Reparatus in Orleansville, Algeria. This small etched labyrinth bears the words 'Santa Ecclesia' at the centre, and there can be little doubt that it was used as an aid to worship and prayer. Its later, and more famous, cousin is to be found in Chartres Cathedral and is thought to date from the thirteenth century. This magnificent labyrinth, with a path over 240 metres in length, stretches right the way across the nave of the cathedral, and once bore a brass or copper plaque at its centre. Sadly, little is written about how it was originally used in terms of meditation or reflection.

The late twentieth and early twenty-first centuries have seen a resurgence in interest in labyrinths as an aid to prayer, and they may be found anywhere from the dusty floor of a community hall to a tent at a Christian festival. They represent a desire to talk to God (or listen to him) while walking. Some years ago a friend of mine designed a multisensory and interactive 'labyrinth' depicting the life of Jesus. At the time it received hundreds of visitors, and has gone on from strength to strength. What started as an experiment in one church hall has now become a fully fledged touring exhibition and can be set up in church halls, schools, community centres and elsewhere. Richard Colpus, the man who designed the 'One Way Experience', says: 'The One Way Experience enables people to walk through scenes from the life of Jesus and encourages them to use all their senses to explore and learn through physical engagement.'[14]

The March for Jesus movement, in the last two decades of the twentieth century, was also all about physical engagement, and represented a very different kind of locomotive Christianity. This was less about meditation and more about declaration.

For some it was underpinned with a deeply embedded sense of territorial spirituality. The marchers saw themselves as reclaiming ground which had been possessed by the forces of evil, whether made manifest in the occult, drug-taking, or deprivation and fractured lives. However it was perceived, it saw tens of thousands of Christians around the world experiencing God on the move as they worshipped, prayed and sang on the streets together. Years later, another marching movement would follow in its wake: Make Poverty History in 2008 saw Christians taking to the streets to walk their faith and parade their concern for inequalities in the world. Theirs was a broad coalition, led by Christians but joined by those who were not who were nonetheless happy to march beneath the campaigning banner.

The increasing popularity of Celtic expressions of Christianity has connected people with the physical environment in an altogether gentler way. People have been drifting back to the rugged places of Celtic Christianity to experience God in the crash of the wave or the hiss of the wind through the heather. Not only that, but many have abandoned their cars in order to do so – walking across the sands at low tide or the hills in the worst of the elements to reach their spiritual destination. With every footstep the life of prayer has been taken away from the bedside or the pew and into the wider world. Simon Reed, joint Guardian of the Community of Aidan and Hilda, captures some of this in an address to the community entitled 'Flame and Struggle':

> It offers a re-imagining of what it means to be a Christian in the twenty-first century – reconnecting the Scriptures and the Spirit, the saints and the streets, the seasons and the soil. We are a people led by a vision which is electrifyingly expressed in the words of the First Voyage of the Coracle: 'God is giving you a vision of a

spoiled creation being restored to harmony with its Creator, of a fragmented world becoming whole, of a weakened church being restored to its mission, of lands being healed and lit up by the glorious Trinity.'[15]

Thus understood, walking and praying is not an escape from the world but a purposeful mission into it.

The 'new monastic' movement has been built on the foundations of Celtic Christianity, with its understanding of God in the rhythms of the natural world. It has also sought to retain some of the accountability, community and discipline which underwrote the monastic life. What makes it *new* monasticism, though, is that these are scattered communities. A person may be a member of the community of St Hilda, for instance, while travelling to work in the heart of the city of London or while farming sheep on a Welsh hillside. Each is encouraged to observe the rhythms of prayer and the disciplines of the covenanted even while going about the business of their daily lives. In this way many are walking (or running, climbing, cycling) while praying. Nancy Louise Frey, commenting on the lessons learned by those who have completed the Camino, writes that: 'Through the movement of the body, through learning new rhythms and perceiving with all the senses, various meanings of the journey begin to emerge which also relate to the life-worlds of the participants.'[16] It is exactly this heightened awareness and retuning of life's rhythms which many seek through new monasticism. Their lives will not allow them to abandon homes and jobs to live in an enclosed spiritual community, nor to leave those commitments behind in order to make their pilgrimage. They are resolved, though, to find God in the fall of every footstep and to measure their prayers with every stride. We shall discuss this in more detail in Chapter 10.

Mapmyprayer

As already mentioned, during the time I have been writing this book, cycling has become part of my life. It all started with someone lending me their road bike while they went abroad for six months. With some trepidation I tried on the cleated racing shoes, clipped myself into the pedals, and wobbled off into the park. I soon got the hang of it, though, and found myself cycling whenever the opportunity arose. At first I so enjoyed the freedom that I eschewed any kind of odometer or cycle computer. However, once I started training for a 100 km charity ride, it became necessary to track my progress. In this way I could measure the distances I was covering and ensure that I was 'up to the job'. On the day I turned 50 I was presented with a sophisticated GPS-enabled computer. This not only stores all the data about my ride – such as speed, altitude and duration – but allows me to upload it onto a website where I can review the journey too. I can look back to see the journey on the map and see how I did. If I were in serious training (which I am currently not) it would be the perfect tool. As it is, it is a bit of fun for now.

Keeping a prayer journal can be the spiritual equivalent of my ride data. It allows us to look back across our life's journey and see how the ups and downs, twists and turns of the route have affected our spiritual health. Many of those who walk the major pilgrimage routes, such as the Camino de Santiago, journal their experiences. Some do it through a photographic blog as they travel. Others write it up as an illustrated travelogue online after their return. Others still, write a book for publication. Any search of an online bookstore will reveal quite how popular this is. Of course, for some it is the written equivalent of the 'selfie' – 'Look, I've been there and done this.' For others it is something more profound – a cathartic outworking of the lessons they learned, the dangers they faced and the challenges they met. In the act of writing it down, they actually begin the vital process of earthing the lessons learned *on* the road in the life lived *off* it.

You don't need to set off on a pilgrimage before starting such a journal. It may be a very simple tool, consisting of the same questions to reflect back on each day of the spiritual journey:

* What was the highlight of today?
* What was the lowest point of today?
* What did I learn about God today?
* What did I learn about myself today?
* What Scripture verse have I taken to heart today?

Why not start it now?

For Reflection

1. Whereabouts have you experienced awe and the presence of God?
2. Think back to a time when you have walked in order to solve a problem in your mind. What was the problem and how did it help?
3. Take a look at the prayers of Moses during his exodus journey – all the way from the banks of the Red Sea to near the banks of the Jordan. What do you notice about them?
4. Try praying while 'on the move' somewhere this week. Do you pray differently?

Companions by Danielle Somerfield

5

Companions

The film was made one year before I was born, but as soon as I was old enough to hear about it, nothing would do but to see it. Disney's *The Incredible Journey* covers the story of an improbable journey across Canada by a golden retriever, a bull terrier and a Siamese cat. When at last I got to watch it I lapped up every minute of it – every mountain vista, every outbreak of bickering between the three, every enemy vanquished and their shared homecoming. What I didn't appreciate at the time was that the 'journey' motif would underlie so many films, from epics like the *Lord of the Rings* trilogy, to silly comedies like *Rush Hour*. Even films which do not seem to be cast in the journey mould are in fact exactly that. *Saving Private Ryan* is the story of a journey to Normandy in pursuit of a soldier who could be Everyman. *Apollo 13* is as much about loyalty and courage on the journey as it is about space travel.

Early 2012 saw a renewed focus on discipleship within my church. Set within Greater London, we had caught 'Olympic fever' as much as anybody else. I wanted to capitalize on this to help instil a spirit of determination and commitment into everybody's understanding of Christian discipleship. This is when I came across *The Way*, directed by Emilio Estevez and featuring his father, Martin Sheen. It tells the story of a wealthy

Californian ophthalmologist whose wayward son goes off to 'find himself' by walking the Camino de Santiago. He dies on the journey, and his father, Tom, goes out to bring the body home. Instead of doing that, he has the body cremated and walks the entire length of the pilgrimage route so that (the remains of) his son can complete the journey. It proves to be a journey of profound physical and spiritual challenge. The production notes to the film say that: 'While Spain serves as the backdrop, the film's primary theme of self-discovery belongs to everyone from all ages and backgrounds, as does the Camino, which has helped transform the lives of millions of pilgrims for centuries.'[1]

After the film was released, Martin toured the USA addressing audiences, principally made up of young people, about the nature of discipleship, humanity and journey. For me, this is where the fusion of journey, discipleship and pilgrimage began. In an interview about the film, director Emilio Estevez says that Tom (the ophthalmologist who is the main character) 'begins to understand that our whole lives are pilgrimages. He begins to understand that even though we all have to walk our own path alone, you still need others.'[2]

Many of these journey films can trace their insights back to the work of mythologist Joseph Campbell, and his 1949 book *The Hero with a Thousand Faces*.[3] In it he suggests that underlying every great story in every culture around the world is the 'monomyth' of the hero's journey. He identifies eleven stages to that journey, as follows:

- Birth
- Call to adventure
- Receipt of an amulet or token
- Crossing the threshold – from the familiar world of home to the unfamiliar

- Tests and trials
- Helpers or companions
- A climax or battle
- Flight – with the battle done the hero must return home
- Return across the threshold – from the unfamiliar to the familiar
- Elixir – a potion or potent symbol which the hero carries with him into the old familiar world
- Home.

Campbell's insights were developed further by thinkers like Kurt Vonnegut, who described all stories as having an identifiable shape. These concepts were also adopted by great screenwriters like Robert McKee, who has influenced many of Hollywood's great directors and producers. Many of the elements mentioned in the hero's journey above will be familiar from the descriptions of the pilgrim's journey as already described. A key feature of the journey out from the familiar and back to the familiar is the companions who accompany the traveller on the way.

The same could be said of the many works of literature which also echo the monomyth. These stretch all the way back to the tales of Jason and his Argonauts in antiquity to Harry Potter with his faithful companions hunting for Lord Voldemort. We can see it in the simplest children's literature, such as Winnie-the-Pooh setting out on his 'Expotition to the North Pole' with Eeyore and Piglet in tow. We can see it in Kerouac's *On the Road*. The journey may be either made or broken by those who accompany us on it.

Chaucer sets his *Canterbury Tales* firmly within the context of companionship, since the whole collection starts in the tavern where the pilgrims rest before starting their journey. These raucous pilgrims exchange their tales to see who will get their food and lodging for free, before setting off on the road to Canterbury together. To 'shorte with oure weye'[4] they will tell their tales as the journey progresses, to keep each other company. Many centuries before Chaucer's tale, probably sometime in the fifth century, the Irish monk Brendan set sail from County Kerry in his simple coracle on a quest for the 'Isle of Paradise'. The prayer he made before he set out is a thing of beauty:

Shall I abandon, O King of mysteries, the soft comforts of home?

Shall I turn my back on my native land, and turn my face towards the sea?

Shall I put myself wholly at your mercy, without silver, without a horse, without fame, without honour?

Shall I throw myself wholly upon you, without sword and shield, without food and drink, without a bed to lie on?

Shall I say farewell to my beautiful land, placing myself under your yoke?

Shall I pour out my heart to you, confessing my manifold sins and begging forgiveness, tears streaming down my cheeks?

Shall I leave the prints of my knees on the sandy beach, a record of my final prayer in my native land?

Shall I then suffer every kind of wound that the sea can inflict?

Shall I take my tiny boat across the wide sparkling ocean?

O King of the Glorious Heaven, shall I go of my own choice upon the sea?

O Christ, will you help me on the wild waves?[5]

As noble and evocative as the prayer may be, we should not be lulled into thinking that this was a lone quest. Every depiction of St Brendan on his journey depicts him with a boat full of companions. Much of the tale of his travels is taken up with the accounts of how the brothers contended between them on the trials and temptations which beset them on the way. Early on, Brendan addresses them as a company when he instructs them to ship the oars, lower the sail, and trust to God to guide them: 'Fear not, brothers, for our God will be unto us a helper, a mariner, and a pilot; take in the oars and helm, keep the sails set, and may God do unto us, his servants and his little vessel, as he willeth.'[6]

We are not best suited to travelling alone, it would seem.

Biblical Companions

In the Bible's story the new paint is barely dry on the bright flowers and blue sky of new creation before God realizes it would be better enjoyed together than alone. Adam is put to sleep, one of his ribs is removed, God fashions from it a companion for his first human being, and so the shared journey of humankind begins. Even when Adam and Eve subsequently leave the garden, they do it together. When the new creation goes awry and God must start again, he picks Noah as the cipher for new humanity, but allows him to take his wife, and their sons and their wives, with him on the ark which will carry them all to safety. Centuries later, after living in slavery and shame, Moses is summoned to set the people free, but he does it with his brother Aaron by his side. The relationship is not an altogether harmonious one, and there are times when Aaron betrays the trust which his brother puts in him. Such things, though, are almost always part of the shared journey. Later still, some of the great prophets will be asked to do tremendous things, but usually with a companion by their side. Ezekiel will have Gehazi, Elijah will have Elisha as a companion and trainee, and Jeremiah will have Baruch by his side to record his words to the bitter end. Ironically, Baruch is told in Jeremiah 45:5 not to 'seek great things' for himself, and it has ended up being Baruch's actual words which endure down through the centuries.

When the New Covenant comes along, Jesus will call disciples to follow him from the outset of his public ministry. Furthermore, when he sends them out to spread the news of his kingdom and to accept the opposition and indifference which goes along with it, he will send them 'two by two' – a recognition that every hero needs a companion on the journey. This still seems to be in his mind when he looks down from the cross on his grieving mother and his disciple, John. He tells Mary 'Behold, your son' and John 'Behold, your mother' (John 19:26–27 ESV). While this makes no biological sense, it makes perfect theological sense. In those few costly words he establishes the parameters of Christian fellowship, where each belongs to the other and none is expected to make the journey alone.

As the work of building the church gets underway in Acts, we see that people rarely work alone. Peter has John, and Paul has various companions, including Barnabas, Luke (who then wrote about their travels) and John Mark. The latter is a good example of how the course of companionship does not always run smoothly. Mark turned back from his first mission trip with Paul, causing the apostle to dismiss him as unreliable despite Barnabas' entreaties. That said, towards the end of his life Paul sent for young Mark, describing him as needed for his work: 'Get Mark and bring him with you, because he is helpful to me in my ministry' (2 Timothy 4:11).

On the journey of faith, God has made us as co-dependent creatures, even if that co-dependency sometimes spills over into disappointment and dismay.

Pilgrim Companions

In its heyday, the pilgrimage routes of Europe were busy with pilgrims from many countries criss-crossing to the different holy sites. They had come from different towns and villages, represented different social classes, and were of different nationalities. The pilgrim road became a kind of melting pot where this diverse group learned to share the same road as they pitted themselves against the elements and the distance. Margery Kempe, from whom we shall hear more in Chapter 11, was an enthusiastic pilgrim in the early part of the fifteenth century. Her book describes her many travels, and throughout them she is dependent on the kindness of strangers: 'Then they went on day by day and met many excellent people. And they didn't say a bad word to this creature, but gave her and her man food and drink, and the good wives at the lodgings where they put up laid her in their own beds for God's love in many places where they went.'[7]

The companionship of the road always seems to have a special quality about it, and relationships forged there can be unforgettable. When Martin Sheen first travelled segments of the Camino de Santiago in preparation for *The Way*, he did it in the company of his grandson, Taylor. Along the way Taylor met his future wife, Julia, at a pilgrim's hostel – which Sheen describes as a miracle.

In many ways, all the things which were true of diverse Christian fellowship were made manifest on the physical road of pilgrimage. Just as the New Testament church had brought Jews and Greeks, slaves and slave-owners together, so both a lord and his labourer could find themselves making the same pilgrimage. On the road, as in church, their shared calling obliged them to tolerate each other. In Chapter 6 you will meet Aymeric Picaud, a papal emissary who travelled the Camino in the twelfth century and then wrote up his travels for submission to the Pope. Bound into the back of his volume, the Codex Calixtinus, are examples of the earliest polyphonic songs to be found anywhere in Europe. Could it just be that the busy pilgrim road – where rich and poor, French, Spanish, English and others walked together – was also the place where people learned to combine their voices as they sang in harmony? Instead of singing in unison, as had always been the habit before, their voices ascended in a newly forged harmony – forged of their shared experiences. However, it was not all about harmony. The exigencies of the long trip on the road would stretch tolerance to the limit. Far from sharing space on a pew once a week, they would have to share road space, sleeping quarters, and even scarce resources of food and drink.

Those who have walked the great pilgrim routes testify to a fluctuating relationship with their fellow travellers. Sometimes they are glad of their company, finding that the long monotony of the miles can be relieved by hearing their stories and learning about their lives. Not only that, but on the harder stretches of the route where a dark forest closes in overhead or the unremitting rain hammers down, some company can be a relief. Fellow companions can provide protection from enemies, encouragement when the road seems long, and even a supporting shoulder when the miles begin to take their toll.

At other times, though, the company can simply be too much. The foibles of the 'other' simply become another burden to bear. Jack Hitt comments on how hard it can actually be to walk together: 'We try to walk together at times, but it never works out. The pace and timbre of one's step on a long haul has a unique quality, like a fingerprint. Each of us moves at our own speed and in our own style.'[8]

Robert Mullen, for whom the Camino was an altogether positive experience, nonetheless comments that being so long 'overlooked by others' was a trial.[9] A common thread in almost all 'journey' literature, whether specifically about pilgrimage or not, is that appreciation of one's travelling companions can wax and wane as the journey progresses. Often it begins with relief that the traveller is not alone, followed by surprise at the tales of others, and intrigue to know more. However, as mile follows mile, that intrigue can turn to frustration and leave the traveller screaming within for a renewed acquaintance with their own company. Occasionally, before journey's end, that frustration gives way to a kind of melancholy, as each traveller realizes that the end of the road will bring about the end of their temporary alliance.

Life on the pilgrim trail was a life lived in company, whether welcome or not. Home was far away, the destination was still far out of sight, and the pilgrim did not get to choose their own company. As much as familiar landscapes had been supplanted with unfamiliar ones, the same could be said of faces. These new companions, with their strange accents, irritating habits and competing demand for hospitality and space, were there for the duration.

Church Companions

Within the Christian church, we are on a shared journey. In her excellent book on medieval maps and pilgrimage, Lisa

Deam comments that: 'Our pilgrimages are as different as we are from one another – as different as our faces, our dreams, and the particular struggles we encounter on our journey through life.'[10] We have come from different backgrounds – rich, poor, and everything in between. The places we have left behind us are all different too. Some have eased into the journey, barely noticing it has begun. For others, there has been a dramatic severance from the past. Now, though, we all share the same road and our hearts are set on the same destination. This is the reason why the pilgrim motif has been so popular with the ecumenical movement, since it sees our differences subsumed by our shared purpose. When the Swanwick Declaration was signed on 4 September 1987 by representatives of many denominations, it declared that the signatories, and the churches which they represented, were 'no longer strangers, but pilgrims':[11]

> This is a new beginning. We set out on our further pilgrimage ready to take risks and determined not to be put off by 'dismal stories'. We resolve that no discouragement will make us once relent our avowed intent to be pilgrims together. Leaving behind painful memories and reaching out for what lies ahead, we press on towards the full reconciliation in Christ of all things in heaven and on earth, that God has promised in his Kingdom.[12]

In some denominations, the emphasis on companionship in faith is particularly strong. Methodist churches traditionally held a 'class meeting' each week, where Christians could sit alongside each other and ask, without fear of censure, 'How is it with you and God this week?' Many independent churches operate a church covenant, where members will sign an agreement binding them to 'walk together' and to 'watch over one another'. This covenantal strand is particularly strong in the Baptist tradition.

Some years ago I was asked if there was any one hymn which was typically Baptist. My mind went straight to the hymn 'Blessed be the tie that binds'. The hymn's writer, John Fawcett, had been the pastor of Hebden Bridge Chapel, in Yorkshire, for seven years. He was then called away to a big church in London. On the day of his last service at Hebden Bridge, as he made his way out to the wagon piled high with his goods, he was overwhelmed by the grief and sorrow of his congregation at seeing him go. At once he ordered that the bags should be unpacked, and he stayed at the church for many more years. Looking back on the experience he wrote his famous hymn:

> Before our Father's throne,
> We pour our ardent prayers;
> Our fears, our hopes, our aims are one,
> Our comforts and our cares.
>
> We share our mutual woes,
> Our mutual burdens bear;
> And often for each other flows
> The sympathizing tear.[13]

What the pilgrims experience once in a lifetime on the road, Christians in fellowship with each other live day by day. Thrown together by their common calling, drawn onwards and upwards by their common hope, they must bear each other's burdens and tolerate each other's weaknesses until the journey is over. This companionship, and the tolerance which makes it possible, may be experienced in numerous aspects of the church's corporate life. The most obvious is worship, where Christians join together in a collective act of praise which overrides their personal preferences. The noisy hand-raiser may stand alongside the quiet head-bower, but both are caught up in an act of transcendent praise which may iron out their differences.

When Christians leave the confines of their own church walls to serve others, their differences appear to take on a different perspective. I remember on one occasion spending part of a night shift with a team of Street Pastors, serving the clubbing and pubbing public of a nearby town. Walking the streets late at night, talking to the sober and drunk alike, all identifiable by our identical high-visibility jackets, the question of differences in churchmanship did not even arise. Missionaries in challenging situations abroad have often found that the differences of tradition and denomination from which they come somehow never make it into their luggage. Instead a new kind of companionship is forged in the face of adversity.

Communal prayer may have a curiously levelling effect upon our companionship too. Faced with an overwhelming need which demands our prayers, the awareness of our own differences fades into obscurity. Those who have attended large prayer meetings at times of crisis will know exactly how that feels. Of course, the way that we choose to pray may present a challenge to our companionship. On one occasion I spent a very pleasant afternoon with a group of Indian pastors, and was delighted when one of them suggested that we should pray together. What I was not expecting was that we would all do it simultaneously, all out loud! My surprise, of course, is part of the richness and risk of diversity.

As those who embark upon a journey of faith, we depart from many different points. We carry many different kinds of baggage and wear many different kinds of outfits for the journey. Like pilgrims on the great pilgrimage trails across Europe, though, we may well find that our paths converge and we end up more reliant on each other than we had expected to be.

For Reflection

1. If you were going to go on a pilgrimage right now, who would your ideal companion be, and why?
2. Can you describe an instance where a companion has made you stronger in your faith, and one where they have made you weaker?
3. Take a look at the story of Naomi and Ruth, especially in Ruth chapter 1. What makes Ruth a good companion?
4. Can you list four or five 'rules of good companionship' for the journey of faith?

Distractions by Ashley Fitzgerald

6

Distractions

Of all the many books about journeys that I have read, Bill Bryson's *A Walk in the Woods* might just be my favourite. In it he sets out with a companion to walk the entire 2,168-mile length of America's Appalachian Trail. Along the way he learns a lot about outdoor skills, about how to pare down the contents of his rucksack, and about himself. In Chapter 3 I shared with you the funny tale of his first morning on the trail. It didn't take him and his companion long to discover that they had packed far too many things in their rucksacks and some of it just had to go. The most poignant lesson, though, is about getting lost. At one point he wanders off the trail and gets separated from his companion. Despite his usual witty style, you can feel the panic rising as he struggles to find his way back to the path and his friend. On a long journey across barren lands, getting lost can be not just inconvenient but dangerous.

We have already talked about the codification of pilgrim law which arose during the Middle Ages. These rules governing the clothing and conduct of pilgrims served not only to keep them safe, but to pave the way for the international laws of today. However, there were other rules which were nothing to do with the countries through which the pilgrims passed. These were unwritten rules governing everything from possessions and sleeping spaces to keeping on track. A pilgrim who stole someone else's sleeping spot could sow a discontent which would rankle in the lodges for days on end. Equally, a pilgrim who wandered off the agreed path and began to trespass on private land could bring all his fellow pilgrims into disrepute. In fact, such abuses could jeopardize the entire pilgrimage. Keeping each other 'on the path' was actually in everybody's best interests.

The Language of Law

We have talked extensively about how the image of journey inhabits the pages of Scripture. It is there, from Noah crossing the angry sea to Moses crossing the Red Sea. It is there, from the magi following the star to the disciples following Jesus. It is there, too, as the apostles set out to cross borders and oceans in pursuit of their mission. Few of these journeys, though, are without rules.

When Noah set out he obeyed all his instructions to the letter about how to build his preposterous ark. Under the watchful glare of his disbelieving neighbours he built a vessel about 135 metres long, 23 metres wide and several storeys high. He boarded it when God told him to and left it when God told him to. Reading the story recently with a group of teenagers, they were overawed by the extent of the man's unquestioning obedience. Such a gargantuan undertaking would have been impossible without God's express instructions. That said, he soon forgot about the rules once the ark made landfall, and paid the penalty.

When Abram set out from Haran at the age of 75, it was on the express understanding that he would do so under God's direction. His frequent sacrifices were much more than 'pit stops' along the way. Instead they served as reminders of God's faithfulness and his own instructions that Abram should trust God and obey his commands to the letter along the way. His success in doing so, though, was far from complete. No sooner had he reached Egypt on his travels than he veered away from the path of promise on which he had been set. Fearing for his safety, he concocted a story about his wife Sarai being his sister, causing no end of suffering to his temporary Egyptian hosts. After Abram would come Jacob, whose path also ran far from smooth. He would start his life struggling with his twin brother, cheat him out of his own birthright for the price of a hot meal, and later fall out with his uncle Laban. Some of his own negative experience of family life would come out in the favouritism and folly with which he would treat his own sons.

Later would come Moses, leaving the comforts of the royal palace and the comforting obscurity of shepherding for a key role in the history of salvation. The giving of the law at Mount Sinai was a reminder that this was to be God's journey, following God's route and abiding by God's rules. A look at any Old Testament Bible map will show you that this was not entirely successful. The so-called 'wilderness wanderings' are but an adventure 'off-piste' writ large. Those who would make the journey of faith are in constant danger of distraction.

In the early days of Christ's ministry, as he gathered enthusiastic crowds around him, the danger was not so much distraction *on* the journey as distraction *from* it. A rich young man had to part from his money, a dutiful young man had to part from his family obligations, and a fisherman had to leave his livelihood behind. It is interesting to note that even after all the miracles they have witnessed, the disciples are found after Easter back at the nets which they know so well. The gravitational pull away from the path of discipleship is strong. Of course, there is nothing inherently wrong or bad about the comforts of home. However, once the call to depart is issued, they can become a dangerous distraction from the task at hand.

In the New Testament era after the ascension we find this again and again. Paul must ask the believers in Galatia not to 'become weary in doing good' (Galatians 6:9). The writer to the Hebrews must urge them 'not [to] give up the habit of meeting together' (Hebrews 10:25 GNT), as some are doing, and to 'strengthen your feeble arms and weak knees' (Hebrews 12:12). Christ's letters to the seven churches are a litany on the dangers of distraction. Ephesus is warned not to 'forsake their first love' (see Revelation 2:4). Sardis is warned to 'wake up' (Revelation 3:2) and not be caught napping, and Laodicea not to be 'lukewarm' (Revelation 3:16). These are all churches which started well and failed to finish – a constant danger for anybody on the journey of faith.

More Starting Than Finishing

The Bible abounds with examples of those who begin the journey of faith but seem in danger of not completing it. Ruth and Orpah are a fine example of this. With their husbands dead, they both nobly offer to return to their mother-in-law's country of birth to keep her company. This was no small thing. Both would have stood out by their accent and looks. They would have stood out as strangers from the very outset. Ruth, of course, completes the journey, but Orpah turns back before they reach the border.

She is not the only one. In the days of Moses, with all the flurry of excitement at the lifting of their bonds of slavery, you would have thought that everyone would have packed their bags and headed for freedom without a moment's hesitation. Actually, it was not long before the people were gazing longingly back over their shoulders at what they had left behind, and asking Moses why he had 'brought [them] to the desert to die' (Exodus 14:11). A journey which started with such promise and excitement soon palled as the miles passed. Again and again the people would complain – about the length of the journey, the food they had on offer, their thirst and their leaders. After Moses' death, Joshua took on the task of leading the recalcitrant people. At the River Jordan, the very edge of the promised land, there were two and a half tribes (Reuben, Gad and half of Manasseh) who did not wish to cross. In the end, it was agreed that their wives and families would settle east of the Jordan, and that the fighting men would join in the conquest of the promised land before returning to them. Further down the road, when the people had been in exile for so many years, at last the time came for them to return to their ancestral homes. We are told in both 2 Chronicles and Ezra that not all of them did, some having been distracted by the life they had forged in exile.

Centuries later, John records an episode in his gospel where Jesus is teaching great crowds around the Sea of Galilee. After feeding five thousand people and crossing the lake on foot, he finds the crowds as big as ever. However, once he starts to spell out what is expected of them and where the journey of discipleship will take them, it is a different story altogether. The crowd thins out, and even the disciples are doubtful. John writes that: 'From this time many of his disciples turned back and no longer followed him' (6:66). As with Orpah and Naomi, some found that the journey of great faith was one easier started than completed.

The story was no different in the New Testament church, with people constantly chipping away at the demands of an exclusive and wholehearted commitment to Jesus as if something else were possible or preferable. Paul was forever trying to stem the tide of those who would divert from the path of discipleship. The Judaizers wanted to revert to Judaism, the antinomians wanted to slink away into lawlessness, and others quite simply ran into the sands of temptation. Some, not surprisingly, feared the wrath of the emperor. Since he believed himself to be divine, the Christian's belief in the divinity of Christ was an act of treason punishable by death. The act of apostasy was treated as unforgivable in the early church, since those who had once renounced their allegiance to Christ could not be relied upon to take it up wholly again. To start the journey of faith courageously was no guarantee of finishing it in a similar way.

Once again, the seven letters to the churches in Revelation stand as testament to this. These had started out as strategic churches in the very cradle of civilization, and should have been the apple of God's eye. However, all but one of them are failing to deliver on their promises of faithful obedience. Some have given in to laziness, some have succumbed to sin, others have lost their first love or fallen into a kind of torpor. None of the churches described in those letters abides, and they stand as a lasting reminder of how easy it is to start well and finish badly . . . or not at all.

Pilgrims

For the pilgrim leaving home to cross the oceans or the continent of Europe, the temptations and distractions would be many. In 1331 Guillaume de Deguileville had a vision of a man whose heart was set on making the pilgrimage to Jerusalem. In the dream a woman (whose name later proved to be 'Grace') warned him of the trials to come: 'To get there you must cross the great sea. The great sea is the world, and it is full of many troubles, tempests and torments, great storms and winds.'[1]

As the excitement of leaving home gave way to the prospect of days without number tramping the pilgrim's path, fatigue would soon set in. It is notable how many modern accounts of pilgrims walking the Camino de Santiago dwell at some length on the physical discomforts. It takes a strong stomach to read all the accounts of blisters and their patent remedies! This is so even with modern lightweight, breathable boots, high-tech woven socks, packable waterproofs and ergonomic rucksacks. What the medieval pilgrim would have given for even a fraction of that equipment!

Other problems included the difficulty of eating strange foods and drinking water from sources of which the pilgrim could not be sure. Twelfth-century writer Aymeric Picaud dwelt on such things with considerable relish in his account, making no attempt to disguise his disgust at some of the local cuisine: 'All kinds of fish, beef and pork in Spain and Galicia make foreigners ill.'[2]

Of course, the problems were not purely physical. Too much time in one's own company, especially in a strange and unforgiving environment, is likely to make anyone prone to self-doubt. Simon Armitage, walking not the Camino but the Pennine Way, talks about this: 'The melancholy comes over me again, the dismal misery of not knowing where I am, or perhaps losing any sense of who I am, as if the mist is bringing about an evaporation of identity.'[3]

Pilgrims on the longer routes, even in the modern era, tell tales of strange encounters bordering on the supernatural, which can terrify a vulnerable spirit. The *Meseta*, or wild plains, section of the Camino de Santiago is especially challenging. Here the pilgrim encounters a flat landscape stretching off as far as the eye can see, with little more than an occasional stunted tree for cover. Add to this the extremes of weather building up over a landmass, such as relentless heat or violent electrical storms, and the temptation to turn back can be enormous. Medieval pilgrims might well have clutched their scallop shell a little tighter at such a moment and prayed for St James himself to intervene on their behalf.

They had to contend not only with fears, but also with temptations. Far away from the soggy shores of England, for instance, who would not have felt at times overcome by the warm sun and luxuries which France and Spain could offer? The scope for over-indulgence in food and wine was considerable, and many a poor pilgrim fell prey to those who had got him drunk only to relieve him of his few possessions. Others found that the warmth of the welcome in some of the hostelries along the way made them forget the arms and hearts of those whom they had left at home. With no one apart from fellow travellers whom they would not meet again to censure them, they were freer than they had ever been before.

A Slope More Than a Cliff

Temptations, or at least our inclination to give in to them, are rarely sudden. We slide into them, rather than falling into them, despite what the phrase about 'falling into temptation' might imply. Consider, for example, King David and his sin of stealing another man's wife and then having her husband murdered. There were several stages between spotting Bathsheba bathing through his palace window and hearing the news that her husband was dead. He could have looked away. He could have had her brought into the palace but then sent her away before any sin was committed. Even once adultery was committed, the sin of murder could still have been avoided. So often our slide into temptation follows a familiar pattern:

- **Opportunity** – the opportunity to sin presents itself, and we must decide whether to seize it or not.
- **Investigation** – instead of walking away, we decide to investigate a little further, despite our declared intention not to get involved.
- **Commitment** – the point at which we have gone past the point of no return.
- **Concealment** – the ways in which we compound the original misdeed by our attempts to conceal it.

Before we know where we are, like a pilgrim wandering off the path and succumbing to temptation in a wayside lodge, the call of the road seems to be replaced by altogether more seductive music.

Churches and the 'D' Word

Churches are collections of people who have opted for the journey of faith. Like the pilgrims of old they have chosen to leave behind familiar ways and head for higher climes. As we have seen in the previous chapter, they walk together, whether closely or loosely. There will be times, though, when someone will wander off the path. Too discouraged to continue, lured down a side road to something that looks a little more attractive, or simply taking up what seems like a better offer – it is bound to happen.

There are numerous things which churches can do about this. At the mildest end of the spectrum is the commitment to pray for each other. We may do so even without knowing the details of what is going on in each other's lives. However, knowing for ourselves how easy temptation comes, it gives us the means to pray for our fellow travellers. Often this level of concern is expressed in a small group of some kind, such as a homegroup. In such a context people can learn to trust each other enough to share their successes, failures, challenges and hopes.

Taking things up another level, we might choose to make enquiries about how things are going. While I have been writing this book I have fallen rather in love with a little wooden triangle. It comes as part of a set of three 'Lifeshapes' – reminders about the essence of discipleship. The three little points of the triangle remind me about three dimensions of my life as a Christian believer – relating *up* to God, *in* to the fellowship of his church and *out* to the world. With one or two trusted friends I can pass the triangle round and ask them, 'How's it going with the up, the in and the out?' In the context of a church leadership team we have found this to be an exceptionally valuable tool, whose usefulness is belied by its simplicity. Together, we have committed to serve God in both discipleship and leadership. Asking one another questions about how things are going in these three dimensions has proved to be a valuable tool in keeping each other 'on track'.

When that kind of 'horizontal' enquiry doesn't work, sometimes it takes a person who is perceived as having some kind of spiritual authority to ask them. A person who will take no notice when a friend warns them that they are straying from the path may listen differently when a church leader or priest says the same thing. In my own ministry it is rare that such a thing will happen, but on a very few occasions it can help. The perception of this varies enormously depending upon denominational background. In essence there is a 'sliding scale' of authority relating to church leadership, with church leaders seen as everything from fellow traveller at one end to spiritual arbiter at the other.

When a person fails to heed the advice of their friends or the concern of their pastor or priest, church discipline may be used as a last resort. In such a case the person may be excluded from certain elements of the church's life or asked to leave the church altogether. This probably has a lot less impact now than it might have had in the days when the next church was a day's journey or more away. For the most part, we only tend to hear about this in high-profile cases now where a well-known pastor is asked to leave office. One of the effects of this is that we regard the whole thing as associated with public scandal, and therefore refuse to countenance it in less drastic circumstances. It is a sad thing, but like a pilgrim shouting 'Don't!' as his new friend tosses the scallop shell in the gutter and turns off the way, it may be the only thing to do.

Remembering the Way Without and Within

Many who have experienced pilgrimages will talk about two journeys taking place at once. The outer journey takes place with every single step on the road. It is felt with every blister, with every twinge of an aching knee, with every squint towards the horizon for the next stopping place. Its path is marked by physical signs, such as the scallop shells which mark the 800 miles of the Camino de Santiago. Pete Stanford writes that the 'origins of the word "travel" in travail, or work, suggest that it should not be the effortless cruise or the door-to-door service of holiday company brochures but rather a sustained and purposeful effort'.[4]

At the same time another, inward, journey is unfolding. This might be a journey away from the familiar and into some kind of promised land. It might even be a journey away from mistakes which have plagued us in the past as we seek some form of absolution. Robert Macfarlane talks about pilgrims walking the Camino where 'every footfall is doubled, landing at once on the actual road and also on the path of faith'.[5] As discussed in Chapter 4, very few journeys take place in one dimension only. However conceived, the rules of the road are intended to ensure that both journeys, the inner and the outer, can be completed without losing your way.

Following the Code

Some years ago I wrote and delivered a discipleship course, drawing on the insights of pilgrimage, upon which much of this book is based. When looking at the issue of distraction, we looked at the British Countryside Code, as written in 2004. This is a simple set of rules governing the safe enjoyment of, and passage through, the countryside for all. It was intended to protect both the rights of landowners and the interests of those who enjoyed the countryside for leisure. Originally drafted as a quaintly named 'code of courtesy' in the 1930s, it has been through various iterations before arriving at its current form. It now has five key points, as follows:

- Be safe – plan ahead and follow any signs.
- Leave gates and property as you find them.
- Protect plants and animals, and take your litter home.
- Keep dogs under close control.
- Consider other people.

These are very simple rules, but between them they represent an aspiration for the preservation of the countryside and the protection of those who pass through it. After briefly studying this code, participants on the discipleship course were then invited to devise a 'disciple's code' for those making the journey of faith. Their suggestions make for interesting reading:

- Be aware of temptation.
- Seek another Christian to confide in.
- Don't stray off the path, but if you do it's never too late to go back to it.
- Be assured that you never walk this way alone.
- Read your guidebook.
- Travel light, making choices about what you leave behind.
- Follow the signs.
- Consider others.
- Stay focused.
- Trust God – you'll get there eventually.
- Remain aware of the world; do not hide away from it.

I wonder what you would have put on the list?

For Reflection

1. Have you ever been away on a holiday where you really did not feel like coming back home? Why?
2. At what point does temptation stop being predictable and start being dangerous?
3. Read the story of King David's temptation in 2 Samuel 11:1–14. At what point could he have stopped?
4. Write your own 'disciple's code'.

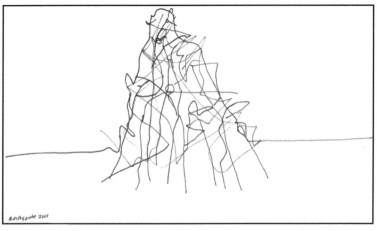

Journey's End by Ashley Fitzgerald

7

Journey's End

Like it or not, this was a journey thick with irony. I was on my way back from a meeting where I had been recruited to serve on the council of a global mission network. Between them the members reached to missions work in just about every continent. I was probably thinking all about that just as sleep overcame me. By the time I woke up, the train had reached its destination in my home town, and was part way through its cyclical journey back into London. One way and another it was an inauspicious start.

Despite what we have said about Campbell and the hero's journey, essentially pilgrimage was *not* cyclical. Instead it was a journey from the familiar to the unfamiliar; from home to somewhere else; from the ordinary to the sacred. Consider this description by Bunyan of Christian's arrival near the city:

In this country the sun shineth night and day: wherefore this was beyond the Valley of the Shadow of Death, and also out of the reach of Giant Despair; neither could they from this place so much as see Doubting Castle. Here they were within sight of the city they were going to; also here met them some of the inhabitants thereof; for in this land the shining ones commonly walked, because it was upon the borders of heaven.[1]

Many weary pilgrims must have felt a similar elation as they drew near to their destination. As the pan-tiled roofs of Santiago de Compostela or the mighty towers of Köln or Canterbury Cathedral came into sight, their hearts must have leapt. Pilgrims arriving in the English cathedral city of Hereford would make straight for the Mappa Mundi, thought to have hung in a side chapel when it was first created around the year 1300. This remarkable circular map depicts 420 cities and has over 500 drawings. Significantly, though, the image of the city of Hereford itself is all but obliterated. This is thought to have been caused by hundreds upon hundreds of pilgrims placing their index finger on the spot as if to confirm that they had finally reached journey's end.

The Codex Calixtinus was a twelfth-century account of a pilgrimage far away from Hereford. The work consisted of five parts. The first three were all to do with St James, the fourth recounts a story of Charlemagne, and the fifth could maybe claim to be the oldest tourist guide in Europe. It gives pilgrims on their way to Santiago advice on everything from where to stay and what to eat, to those places at which they could most safely cross each river in their path. Along the way it has some pretty stern words about those who prey upon the pilgrims by exacting tolls from them. The writer says that any bishop choosing to pardon such a person should be 'kicked out of the church'.[2] On arrival at the city, the writer gives advice about where to go and what to do in order to ensure the proper completion of the pilgrimage. He even describes the souvenir stalls behind the cathedral in a little square with a fountain: 'Here are sold the shells which are the badges of St James, and also wineskins, shoes, deerskin scrips, purses, thongs, belts, all kinds of medicinal herbs, and other drugs, and much else besides.'[3]

Pilgrims touching the Mappa Mundi in Hereford and others buying a new deerskin scrip in Santiago were all celebrating the same thing – journey's end.

Arriving dirty, ragged, hungry and footsore, it must have been very overwhelming. If you look carefully at the figure on the cover of this book, you will see that there are tufts of wool protruding from the huge timbers from which the man is constructed. Artist Glenn Morris embedded them there as a homage to the sheep farming which for centuries has been a feature of the landscape where the statue stands. However, from a distance it looks as though the pilgrim's garments have been torn away by wind and weather. Often a pilgrim's clothes – washed again and again and exposed to wind, sun and rain along the way – are doing just that by the time journey's end comes. Many pilgrims, both sacred and secular, talk of a kind of ecstatic state which transcends their fatigue. Even Jack Hitt, with his resolutely secular agenda, talks about his transcendent experience on arriving in Santiago: 'I hear them talking of me, as a true pilgrim – a dirty, ugly, filthy, smelly pilgrim. It's a queer kind of celebrity. Yet every pilgrim wants some sense of confirmation from without.'[4]

When at last medieval pilgrims arrived at the cathedral of Santiago, many would make their way up the stairs at the West Door on their knees. There is a column at the top of these stairs which now bears forever the handprint of all the pilgrims who have gratefully grasped it so near to the end of their journeys. From there, they would proceed to the statue of St James himself, often embracing it and whispering a prayer of thanks for their safe arrival. Some might 'hug the apostle' for those who had helped them on their way – by providing food or lodging – and ask for a favour from the apostle by way of recompense. Most pilgrims would then collect their *compostela* or certificate of proof that they had completed the pilgrimage. Afterwards they would climb out onto the roof of the cathedral to the Cruz dos Farrapos, or 'Cross of Rags'. Here their filthy garments could be burned, and the cathedral chapter would provide clean ones to wear instead.

Dying to Get There

Having traced the parallels between the pilgrim's journey and the Christian's journey, it is hard not to see parallels here with dying. After all, that is where our journey with Christ, insofar as we understand it, comes to an end. After that comes our arrival at the city of the New Jerusalem, where we shall be provided with clean white robes to wear and all evidence of the old world goes up in flames. After that, words themselves are incapable of describing what will be.

When I came to teach a course on discipleship for 2012, I found that none of the available material covered the matter of dying. This seemed crazy to me, when dying is surely the one experience which is common to every Christian of every nationality and every denomination. Why do we not talk about this? Since we are saved for all eternity, one could even say that our whole lives are spent *preparing* to die. It strikes me that every pilgrim must have talked about their destination as they fell in with others along the way. There must have been talk about how it would be, what sights they would see, what prayers they would hope to see answered when they got there. For those who had undertaken their pilgrimage as a form of penance, there must have been the delicious anticipation of a burden lifted and the prospect of walking tall once more.

As a pastor now for over twenty-five years, I am amazed by how seldom Christians talk about dying. We even avoid the word itself. Instead we talk about 'passing away', 'going to be with the Lord' or 'slipping away'. It is as if we are embarrassed to mention the very thing which has been on the horizon ever since we signed up for this journey of faith. This should not be so, surely? As a young pastor I can recall making my final visit to a Christian woman in hospital. I had been summoned in, as her breathing was shallow and this would be her last night on earth. She was way beyond conversation and slipping in and out of consciousness. I sat with her, held her hand, read a promise or two from Scripture, and prayed for her. After that I slipped away through the darkened ward overwhelmed with one emotion above all others. That emotion, to my own surprise, was envy. Before I woke the next morning, she would be at journey's end. While I closed my eyes to concentrate on an unseen Jesus the next day as I prayed, she would see him face to face. I was reminded of the line of an old hymn: 'We feebly struggle, they in glory shine.'[5]

Ultimate and Penultimate

Years before I became a pastor I studied Bonhoeffer – a brave and angry young theologian whose theological brilliance shone brightly against the darkness of Nazi Germany. I admired him for his courage and his intellectual rigour. His deep convictions led him to return from a safe job overseas, teaching in Union Theological Seminary, to share Germany's fate in 1935. Those same convictions would eventually lead to his involvement in the plot to assassinate Adolf Hitler, and would result in his execution. A doctor at the prison camp where he was executed later recorded the moments before his death:

> I was most deeply moved by the way this lovable man prayed, so devout and so certain that God heard his prayer. At the place of execution, he again said a short prayer and then climbed the few steps to the gallows, brave and composed. His death ensued after a few seconds. In the almost fifty years that I worked as a doctor, I have hardly ever seen a man die so entirely submissive to the will of God.[6]

In better days, when he was training pastors, Bonhoeffer had written about the ultimate and the penultimate. The penultimate is where we live now – a place of testing, longing and living by faith. The ultimate is where we shall live then – a place of eternal dwelling in the presence of God. In those moments of the penultimate when our body grows weak or the end looms large, we should draw upon the comfort which the ultimate offers us.

Another German theologian, Alfred Delp, also showed great theological insight in this area. Arrested in July 1944 for his part in the circle of those who knew about the plot to assassinate Hitler but failed to divulge it, he would eventually be executed in February 1945. His writings, smuggled out of Tegel prison in his washing, are soaked through with the theme of advent and the anticipation of better things when this life was ebbing away: 'The terror that accompanies such an awakening to one's own situation is finally and conclusively overcome from within by the certitude that God has already set out and is on His way.'[7] Delp saw each Christian as being on a journey, describing man as 'a wayfarer, a scout, hungering and restless'.[8] That journey could have only one conclusion, and he was confident that God held it in his hands.

When Jacob made his final speech to his assembled family, he talked of being 'gathered to my people' (see Genesis 49:33), expressing his belief that there were better things to come. Paul talks about his desire to 'depart and be with Christ' (Philippians 1:23), and Jesus himself encouraged us to believe that he was 'going ahead to prepare a place for us' (see John 14:2). Joshua, too, talks about going 'the way of all the earth' (Joshua 23:14). Despite the subtle differences in phraseology, these expressions all point in the same direction as they describe the onward journey for the person of faith.

Having the Conversation

For pilgrims travelling together, there must have been practical conversations on the last day or two of their journey about what would happen when they got to the end. Would they sleep when they arrived, and worship the next day? Would they exchange their clothes for clean ones, or were their rags a badge of honour? When at last they came to the shrine, would they approach it upon foot or on their knees? What would their first word be on completion of their sacred journey?

Christians who travel together need to have this conversation about dying. Husbands and wives, children and parents, even best friends, really should talk about what matters. After all, as Evangeline Paterson reminds us in her wonderful poem, we are not sightseers but pilgrims – and our pilgrimage goes only one way:

> I used to think –
> loving life so greatly –
> that to die would be
> like leaving a party
> before the end.
>
> Now I know that the party
> is really happening
> somewhere else;
> that the light and the music –
> escaping in snatches
> to make the pulse beat
> and the tempo quicken –
> come from a long way away.
>
> And I know too
> that when I get there
> the music will never end.[9]

There are numerous resources available to help with such conversations, not least from organizations like Dying Matters. They produce a simple card which encourages people to talk about 'five things to do before I die' and 'five things I want to be remembered for'. These things can be banal or serious, unattainable or ordinary. The main thing is to talk about them. When I made postcards available with these two sets of questions, they were gobbled up without any apparent reticence or embarrassment. Not only that, but when people were invited at the end of a six-week discipleship course to provide feedback, the single session upon which they commented the most was . . . the one on dying. These easier questions may be the precursor to talking about some far harder ones. These may be to do with the physical experience of death: will it hurt and which sensation will I lose first? They may be to do with the immediate family: how ever will you cope? They may reflect back from the moment of dying to the here and now: are there things I should sort out before it is too late?

Since first writing that session on the discipleship course, I have preached on the subject in my own church and elsewhere. One congregation were asked to list their preferred 'hot topics' for preaching, and dying came out as the top one. The pastor then kindly invited me to tackle it! I did so, quoting from Canon Henry Scott Holland's sermon preached after the death of King Edward VII in 1910. His words, 'Death is nothing at all',[10] have often been quoted vastly out of context, since he goes on to say that death is in fact far from that. The initial impression on seeing a person who has just died is that since they look pretty much the same, death is not such a big deal. It is on walking away that the real impact strikes home. As Scott Holland describes it: 'How black, how relentless, this total lack of tangible evidence for the certainty we believe in.'[11] Dying is a fact which is as inevitable as the conclusion of any pilgrim's journey, and we do well to face it squarely and talk about it.

In the years since the course was completed, so-called Death Cafés have been springing up in many towns and cities. These are exactly as they sound – a relaxed, café-style setting where a facilitator allows people to talk about dying. Their own publicity describes them like this: 'At a Death Café people, often strangers, gather to eat cake, drink tea and discuss death. Our objective is "to increase awareness of death with a view to helping people make the most of their (finite) lives"'.[12] People who attend the cafés might want to talk about how it could feel physically, about their choices concerning burial and commemoration, or about their loved ones. Since their inception in 2011, 1,617 of these cafés have been held in the United Kingdom. Whatever the precise topics which people raise over their cup of tea and cake, the main thing is that there appears to be an appetite to talk.

In short, like pilgrims talking about their destination, we need to talk about ours.

For Reflection

1. What worries you most about dying?
2. How would you like to be remembered?
3. When Abraham dies, he is described in Genesis 25:8 as 'old . . . and full of years'. How would you interpret that phrase?
4. Consider Joshua's farewell speech in Joshua 24. What have his years taught him?

A Pilgrimage Lived by Rachel Morris

8

A Pilgrimage Lived

All in all, it was a very foolish enterprise. I had slipped out of my hotel room in Lake Garda intent on taking a gentle stroll around the shore. The trouble is, the heights were calling to me. Looming above the town is a vast rocky outcrop known as 'La Rocca' and I just had to climb it. I wasn't equipped for such a climb, wearing entirely the wrong footwear and not having told a soul where I was going. It took me a while to find the path, after one wrong turning to a small eleventh-century chapel, and another into a person's front drive. At last I found the path behind a row of cottages, and began to climb. Things began well enough, with robust steps cut into the hillside. After the next bend, though, it was a different story. The steps gave way to a smooth, muddy slope, and as it wound up under the treeline it was interlaced with gnarled tree roots just waiting for the inappropriately shod! By the time it got nearer to the top there were caves and gulleys just inches from the edge of the path. At last, the woods gave way to a grassy knoll, and I could look down on the harbour dotted with apparently toy boats, far below. The thing is, I didn't really know what to do next. For the past hour, my mind had been set on reaching the top, but now that I was there I had no goal. I took a few photos and then, stomach rumbling for my breakfast, picked my way down again.

Going Home

Author Nancy Louise Frey has lived much of her life in Santiago, and watched pilgrims come and go by their thousands. Her particular interest, though, is in what they do after the pilgrimage is over. Once the saint is hugged, the compostela is stamped, the rags burned, then what? They cannot return home as a different person; rather they should return home as the same person, but with the old one enriched and deepened, rather than erased. Frey asks the question: 'What happens when the goal is the way and not the shrine, and the end comes while making the journey or after the goal is reached and the pilgrim returns home?'[1]

Almost without exception, accounts of those making the Camino or similar pilgrimages tell us nothing about the journey home. It is as if their creative and spiritual resources have been exhausted by the experience, and they have no more to give. It may also be because their journeys home seem, by comparison, unworthy of comment. The places to which they return and the threads of lives which they pick up on arriving there seem somehow unworthy of comment. This is a loss to everybody, surely? A pilgrimage may take up a few weeks, or even months, of a person's life, but the rest of their lives is lived far away from the wide-open spaces of the pilgrim's journey and the beckoning spire of the cathedral.

One of the more unusual journey books on my shelf is *Moondust: The Men Who Fell to Earth*, by Andrew Smith. In it, he interviews all nine surviving Apollo astronauts who have walked on the moon. For the most part, their re-entry to life on earth was every bit as challenging as their lunar adventure. Returning to planet earth and finding some kind of ordinary existence was beyond most of them. Some became recluses, some became almost obsessive about their lunar experiences, and some became embittered. It was never easy for the second man on the moon, Buzz Aldrin, as you can imagine. Conversely, towards the end of his life the first man on the moon, Neil Armstrong, shunned pretty much all publicity. Alan Bean, who flew on the Apollo 12 mission, has painted and painted and painted his lunar experiences throughout all the years since returning to earth. While this is a positive outworking of the experience, it is nonetheless obsessive, and demonstrates the intensity of the lunar voyage. These men found that their extraordinary experiences made them uncomfortable on returning to the lives they had left behind. As Smith says, 'For me, this is the surprise collective lesson of the Moon men. No-one was changed but everyone was galvanized. Whatever they took with them, they brought back tenfold, like coals crushed to diamond.'[2] They did this with varying degrees of success. Their lives were never the same again, and their extraordinary collective experience is evidence. Coming home is not a simple matter . . .

Villafranca

Villafrance da Buiz is just one of many 'pilgrim' towns which grew up along the end of the Camino. Originally established by monks who had travelled from Cluny to attend to the pilgrims as they passed, it became something more permanent. As the name suggests, this became a French town in Spanish territory. Those who could not or would not return to the life they had left behind took up residence there. In this sense it became a cultural anomaly which owed its very existence to the Camino.

The thing is, we all have an inclination to linger, occasionally too long, at the place where we have encountered the divine in some powerful way. In this way our memories of a powerful spiritual moment may actually impede our progress. We dwell too much upon them, like the Israelites under Moses eating yesterday's hoarded manna, and growing sick as a result. Our memory of a great spiritual event becomes a talisman, rather than a goad towards greater things still. I have witnessed this many times as a pastor when people tell me that they have played the recording of a particular sermon or address time and time again. To do so is to miss the point, surely? When Jesus healed a dangerous demoniac in the region of the Gerasenes, he rejected the man's entreaties to stick close by his healer, telling him instead to: 'Return home and tell how much God has done for you' (Luke 8:39). Maybe this is why Martin Luther King's speech, so forward-looking in every regard, actually urges people to go *back* to the places from which they had come: 'Go back to Mississippi, go back to Alabama, go back to South Carolina, go back to Georgia, go back to Louisiana, go back to the slums and ghettos of our northern cities, knowing that somehow this situation can and will be changed.'[3] The civil rights battle was not going to be won in Washington DC alone, but in every state from which the marchers in the crowd had come. Mountain-top experiences which stay on the mountain will do little to empower life in the valley. Presumably those who settled in the various Villafranca towns never got to tell their tales of provision, protection and enlightenment to those who might have benefited from them the most. Instead, they left people in their towns and villages wondering where they had gone and what might have become of them. In all the pilgrim literature I have read, whether sacred or secular, almost nothing is said about the return journey. At most it receives a paragraph or two tacked on to the end of the book.

Why might this be, I wonder? It may be that the journey home seems too dull and tame compared to what has gone before. Equally, it may be that the writers have quite simply exhausted their creative resources. What is of more concern, though, is that those writing about an overtly spiritual pilgrimage may feel that the life to which they return lacks the spiritual significance of the pilgrim trail. The intensity of both challenge and inspiration they have known on their great spiritual undertaking may make the rest of life seem anodyne and dull by comparison. Like the pilgrims who stopped off in Villafranca and never went home, they want to stay in the place where the sun shines and the bells toll and the monotony they have left behind is but a memory. This is a dangerous trend, since it impoverishes the Christian life lived in our ordinary context rather than investing in it.

Iteration and Realization

A couple of years ago I met someone who described himself as a 'graphic enabler and rich picture artist'. At the time, I had no idea what those titles meant. At its most basic, his job is to listen to people talk and to draw what they say. When he then shows them what he has drawn, they start to think differently about the words they have said and the ideas behind them. Thus, if someone talks to Josh about a roadblock to progress in her business, he might draw exactly that – a roadblock. When the client and her colleagues look at a truck stuck behind the roadblock on the finished piece, they might smile and say 'That truck's a bit like us, really, isn't it?' . . . and so the conversation progresses. Sometimes the process is an iterative one, where the conversation about the truck will lead to insights about what, exactly, is under its wheels. These are then drawn, and discussed . . . and the conversation proceeds from there.

In many ways my intention in focusing on pilgrimage in this book has been exactly the same. I no more expect every reader to embark on a pilgrimage tomorrow than that businesswoman expects to wake up tomorrow and see a cartoon truck in her driveway and a roadblock across the end of it. Rather, I want people to look at their path to work, or to college or to the neighbour's house, as a segment of the pilgrim's way, with all that implies. I want them to consider their life's journey, wherever their feet might take them, as a pilgrim's way – complete with leaving home, provisions, communications, companions, distractions and a journey's end.

Maybe I am calling here for an extended metaphor – the word, after all, means to 'carry with' – the idea being that words paint pictures in our minds which carry us with them into places where we have not yet been. The pilgrim metaphor, upon which we have dwelt over these past few chapters, may carry us with it into new depths and onto new heights in our experience of discipleship. Robert Macfarlane comments that while we 'think in metaphors drawn from place', those metaphors may actually 'not only adorn our thought but actively produce it'.[4] The time we have spent on this pilgrim metaphor is intended not only to give us something to think about, but to produce reflective consideration of our daily discipleship. If I am not walking 800 miles to Santiago, but am walking a few metres into work, how should I do it? If my journey will take me a lifetime, rather than a few months, how can I allow that blend of curiosity and determination to leach back from the pilgrim's path into my own?

Maybe I could think a little harder about the starting line of my faith. How did it feel when I took those first teetering steps away from the village of unbelief, where I had always lived . . . and out into faith? It may be good to dwell just a little longer on those things which I left behind. This is not a nostalgic indulgence, but a necessary backward glance, like checking your rear-view mirror before pulling out into traffic. *Leaving home* is something which every Christian has done, and we do well to remember it. Can we enumerate, for instance, those specific sins and prejudices which we left behind in order to embrace the cause of Christ? Were there particular strangleholds upon us which had to be broken in order for us to 'leave home'? Some may have given up suspicions and prejudices bred into their family line over many generations. Others may have left lucrative incomes or absorbing hobbies on one side because the call of the upward journey was greater. Without acknowledging the pull which these things once had on us, we may find them exerting themselves all over again once the journey is under way.

We should take a long, hard look at our *provisions*, too. Few of us took a vow of poverty when entering the Christian faith. We need to ask, though: do the things which we own help or hinder on the journey of faith? Do they weigh us down and make us slower? The Bible does not, of course, say that money is the root of all evil, rather that the *love* of money can cause us problems. Should we maybe think of lightening the load a little, as every pilgrim must do? Painful though it may be, the time may have come to conduct some kind of audit of our lives. Do we really need all the things which we gather about us? Do they serve any purpose other than to make us feel important? Some of them do, but others surely do not. The weeding out of possessions which happens when we move house need not necessarily wait until then. Picture yourself as a pilgrim, with a long journey on foot ahead of you. What would you leave behind?

Reflecting on our *communications* can only be a good thing. We may feel that God notices when we do not talk to him much, but he is not the only one! When we fall out of touch with him people in every area of our lives are affected. Francis Chan, in his *Basic* discipleship course, says that 'walking is measured not in miles, but in steps'.[5] Maybe we should look a lot harder at the connections between prayer and motion, weaving prayer more into our daily lives than we have done before. Since stillness is in short supply for most of us, we should perhaps investigate a little more how prayer may happen in motion. A church abroad in the world can only be good for the world, but not if it has forgotten how to be the church. If prayer seems less vital than it once did, read some stories of people on long journeys far from home. Hear the pleading in their voices to stay connected to their loved ones. Read some old letters sent from soldiers on the front to families back home. Christian – you need to stay in touch.

Perhaps it is time to take a good look at our *companions*, too. We did not choose them, any more than a pilgrim chooses those with whom he falls in step on the road. However, they are God's provision to us, and we should not take them for granted. A belief in the providence of God would suggest that there is no such thing as an 'accidental' companion, so maybe they all deserve a second look? Many a traveller, or pilgrim, has grown immensely fond of his or her companions by the time journey's end comes around. They may have challenged, grated, infuriated and tried patience to the very limit. Be that as it may, by the end of the journey they have become more precious than anything. The most sceptical writers on pilgrimage, both sacred and secular, seem to end up appreciating their companions more than they would ever have thought possible. During his journey *Around the World in 80 Days*, travel writer

Michael Palin spent one week on a dhow crossing the Arabian Sea. At the end of it he writes: 'So the time comes to say good-bye to the people in whose hands we have entrusted our lives for the past week. It's been a unique relationship, for I can't imagine any other circumstances in which we would have become so close so quickly to people like this.'[6] Maybe it is time we valued our companions on this curious journey a little more.

We have taken account of the traps and *distractions* which have so often beset God's people on the move, whether across the Sinai desert or across the Pyrenees. The traveller most at risk of temptation is the one who thinks that she or he is immune to it. It can be a worthwhile exercise to conduct an 'audit' of our spiritual journey once in a while. Try doing this by plotting an actual timeline of the past few years with the ups and downs labelled accordingly. On the peaks, where you felt close to God, what was making you feel that way? Look at the dips too, when you felt low and far away from God; what else was going on in your life at the time? In the end, most pilgrims prevail against distraction because it is outweighed by the gravitational pull of their desire to complete the sacred journey. Could the same be said for us?

The refusal to think about *journey's end* is one which no pilgrim could afford. For a start, they had to actually know where they were going. Not only that, but the prospect of their glorious arrival would be enough to sustain them on a long and arduous journey. As Christians we have shied away from talking about journey's end, and laid up all kinds of problems for the dying and the bereaved by doing so. It is time we put this right.

To leave on pilgrimage can be an enormous, life-changing, profound and unsettling experience. It can change our perspective on those things which we left behind as well as our focus on the place to which we are heading. Along the way, our possessions, our companions, and even the sound of our own praying voices can sound different. The question is, aren't all these things true of anyone who has embraced the life of faith as a disciple of Christ, intent on following the path and sound of his footsteps?

For Reflection

1. What objects do you have in your possession because they remind you of a spiritual milestone?
2. Revisit the story of the demoniac in Luke 8. Why do you think Jesus would not allow the man into the boat, and how do you think that man felt?
3. Use the timeline approach described above to describe your spiritual journey as far back as you can remember. Where have the highs and lows been, and why?
4. How would you feel about being described as a pilgrim?

The Language of the Road by Richard Littledale

9

The Language of the Road

In the mid-1970s, like lots of other boys my age, I thought CB radio was the coolest thing ever. On one occasion my brother and I were driving along in his car and I was holding an aerial which we were going home to fit. Seeing it poking out of a window, a boy on a street corner shouted out 'What's your handle?' and we were thrilled. CB radio (which I never had, by the way) had a vocabulary all of its own, which would eventually find its way into TV, film and music.

It's the same with other forms of transport. Seafarers have nicknames for different patches of ocean and currents. As a child I had a map of the British shipping areas such as 'German Bight' and 'Dogger' on my wall. To this day, the sound of them being read out on the Shipping Forecast has a somewhat nostalgic effect upon me. However, in truth they mean nothing to me as a non-sailor.

Pilots have a jargon all of their own too. Mountaineers describing ascents to one another use all kinds of terms which make sense only to other climbers. Walkers on long-distance paths may find that they develop a kind of shared vocabulary too. Dips and twists on the path may gain their own 'pet' names, and the words to describe different kinds of conditions along the way may be unique to that particular landscape. In his latest book, *Landmarks*, Robert Macfarlane cites the memoir of a shepherd (Angus MacMillan) on the Isle of Lewis, sent by his father to search for a missing sheep: "'*Cùl Leac Ghlas ri taobh Sloc an Fhithich fos cionn Loch na Muilne*" – "just behind the Grey Ledge by the Raven's Hollow above the Mill Loch". "Think of it," writes MacMillan drily, "as an early form of GPS: the Gaelic Positioning System."[1] Such talk is the language of those who express a relationship with the land alien to most who will read this book, and indeed to the one writing it.

As our lives change, so our language changes with it. Blackberries and apples become something you type on rather than something you pick. The world beyond our settled and urbanized lives slips further and further from our linguistic grasp. A shepherd such as MacMillan seems like a creature from another planet, and we talk of the landscape only in the vaguest of terms. Beyond the cities are 'the hills' and beyond the hills are 'the mountains', but we would be hard pushed to name them. Macfarlane says that this has turned the world beyond the city into a 'blandscape'.[2] In this way a change of language represents a shift in perception, both of the world described and the one describing it.

Pilgrim Language

Pilgrims who had never spoken such words would find themselves talking about scrips, scallops, and staffs. There is also a whole vocabulary which builds up around the road, with pithy descriptions of fellow travellers and shorthand expressions for the traveller's afflictions of foot or stomach. Not only that, but as the end of the journey drew nearer, mention of the much longed-for *compostela* or certificate of completion would be more and more frequent. Even those writers who eschew any kind of spiritual agenda when writing about the Camino end up sounding almost wistful towards the end of their journeys. Consider this, for example, from sceptical *New York Times* journalist Jack Hitt: 'Over time the road takes up residence within us and becomes the way to something else.'[3] When people write like this, it is as if the journey has flowed not only beneath their feet but into their veins.

The word *ultreia* is inexorably linked with pilgrimage in general and the Camino in particular. Nobody seems quite sure when the word came about, nor indeed of its precise origins. Most see it as a Galician word, but note its Latin origins too. We see it below in a French version of a song which has been sung on the Camino for centuries:

> *Tous les matins nous prenons le chemin*
> *tous les matins nous allons plus loin.*
> *Jour après jour la route nous appelle*
> *c'est la voix de Compostelle.*
> *Ultreia, ultreia et suseia*
> *Deus adjuva nos!*[4]

(Translation: Every day we take the road / Every day we go further / Day after day the road calls to us / it's the voice of Compostela. / Onward, onward and follow / God is for us!)

Translations of the word vary from the simple 'onward and upward' to the more complex 'keep going and walk further'. Despite its ancient origins, it still gets used today. People who have walked the Camino de Santiago use it as a sign of recognition and shared experience with others who have done the same. They use it as a kind of shorthand born of shared experience – a language of the road. I have had numerous people send it to me as a greeting as I work on this book. In so doing they have admitted me to a fraternity where I am unsure that I have earned my place. That said, I am honoured all the same.

Bible Language

Language is always the product of its context, and the Old Testament is no exception. Much of the content of the first few books is written in the language of the exodus. This is a language shot through with gratitude and wonder at the escape the Hebrews have experienced from the constraints and horrors of the past. Time and time again God is referred to as the 'God-who-brought-us-up-out-of-Egypt' as if this tells people everything they need to know about his power and character. If the first five books of the Bible were indeed written (or dictated) by Moses, as tradition holds, then it is no wonder that they have such a distinctive 'flavour'. Deuteronomy 8, for example, is a call to faithfulness, but it is couched in the language of the road as it reminds people of the clothes they wore, the provisions they ate, the protection they enjoyed and the sustenance they were given. In a particularly graphic verse they are asked to remember that: 'Your clothes did not wear out and your feet did not swell during these forty years' (v. 4). Significantly, they are told to remember these lessons they learned on the road and under canvas when they 'build fine houses and settle down' (v. 12). This is a warning which many a pilgrim has had to heed since.

After this comes the language of exile, as the sound of the great prophets' voices rises above the hue and cry of life on the margins. This is a language which resounds with a curious combination of nostalgia and urgency. At times it can be like listening to a duet between a cello, with its rich, mellow note . . . and a bugle with its shrill, insistent call to battle. Consider, for example these words penned by a captive in exile:

> By the rivers of Babylon we sat and wept
> when we remembered Zion.
> There on the poplars
> we hung our harps,
> for there our captors asked us for songs,
> our tormentors demanded songs of joy;
> they said, 'Sing us one of the songs of Zion!'
>
> How can we sing the songs of the Lord
> while in a foreign land?
> If I forget you, Jerusalem,
> may my right hand forget its skill.
> May my tongue cling to the roof of my mouth
> if I do not remember you,
> if I do not consider Jerusalem
> my highest joy (Psalm 137:1–6).

In these words there is both longing for a lost past, and resolve to find it once again. To 'sing the songs of Zion' has been a cipher for the experience of displaced people ever since.

In neither of these contexts is it 'settled' language. In the one it is the language of a people shaped by their experience of disconnection – on the move from a land of slavery to a land of promise. Even once they get there, it still infuses their speech and poetry. The language of the exile, on the other hand, is a language of longing. It is rich with the tones of mourning and sadness, forever focused on another place.

When the writer to the Hebrews writes to those who have risked all kinds of opprobrium for turning to Christ, he has much of this in mind. Many were suffering everything from ostracization to physical persecution on account of their loyalty to their Lord. The writer reminds them that they stand in a long tradition of those who don't belong on earth because they already have a foot in heaven:

> They did not receive the things promised; they only saw them and welcomed them from a distance, admitting that they were foreigners and strangers on earth. People who say such things show that they are looking for a country of their own. If they had been thinking of the country they had left, they would have had opportunity to return. Instead, they were longing for a better country – a heavenly one (Hebrews 11:13–16).

If the world was making their lives tough and denying them their rights of citizenship, they should remember that their citizenship in the heavenly country is assured.

As the church became more established and grew out from under the threat of the oppression which had been there for so long, there was a danger that people might forget these transitory roots. They might become more settlers than nomads, and forget that the journey was not only under their feet but in their hearts. Like a Romany buying a house, parking his traditional caravan in its garden, and leaving it until the plants and creepers have overgrown it completely, there is a danger that they should forget who they really are. James reminds his readers that the whole of life is contingent, and they should speak accordingly:

> Now listen, you who say, 'Today or tomorrow we will go to this or that city, spend a year there, carry on business and make money.'

Why, you do not even know what will happen tomorrow. What is your life? You are a mist that appears for a little while and then vanishes. Instead, you ought to say, 'If it is the Lord's will, we will live and do this or that' (James 4:13–15).

This is far more than a kind of playground superstition which says you will fall through the cracks if you don't say the magic words. This is an urgent reminder that the pilgrim dare not forget his or her place. For the Christian believer, infused with the idea of the journey, permanency is an illusion. Like the Indian saying quoted in Chapter 3, this world is 'but a bridge', and we do no more than pass through it. 'Home' may refer in the past tense to those things which we have left behind, or may be a wistful description of what is yet to be, but those who know they are on a journey have no home just now.

Journey Language

Years ago, friends of mine used to work as house parents in a boarding school for the children of missionaries. The children came from many different countries, and now lived in another place altogether. Some only visited the country where they were born, or where their grandparents lived, every few years. In such a context, referred to by professionals as a 'third culture' setting, what was meant by the word 'home'? To refer to the place visited so infrequently as home seemed inappropriate. Equally, all of them knew that their residence in the school, and the country where it was situated, was at best a temporary measure. Language needed to be adjusted in order to accommodate their particular situation. In the end, people would refer to their 'passport country' as a means of describing their nationality – a good example of language adapting to an anomalous situation.

Another example of such a linguistic adaptation would be the presence of British troops in Afghanistan throughout the period of 2005–14. All public references were to a 'mission' rather than an occupation, and the language of impermanence was used throughout. Camp Bastion, with its 26 square-kilometre area and more than 10,000 occupants, was the size of many small towns. However, the soft-sided buildings and the label 'camp' were a reminder that it was never intended to be there forever. Language was adapted to underpin the deeper reality.

Do we need to make a similar adaptation in the Christian church today, I wonder? In my office I have a scruffy, peeling poster framed as a reminder of days gone by. If you look carefully you can see that it has been pasted together with various amendments, and pencilled instructions to the printer. The poster advertised the opening services for Teddington Baptist Church on Sunday 1 April 1884. It bears a description of the time, place, and preacher, followed by the capitalized letters D.V. They meant, of course, *Dieu voulant* (God willing), and expressed a humble belief that even such a grand enterprise as opening a new church was contingent upon the plans and blessing of God.

Today such a thing would seem like an affectation. However, it serves as a reminder that the life of the pilgrim is contingent, tied to the road upon which they walk and the God who called them to do so. Maybe it is time we watched our language a little more?

For Reflection

1. Do you remember nicknames for particular places from the place where you grew up?
2. Can you identify phrases which you would class as 'Christian jargon'?
3. Which words or phrases would you regard as helpful reminders of the disciple's journey?
4. How would you explain those phrases to somebody who had just embarked on the journey of faith?

Scattered Ways and New Monks by Maureen Kerr

10

Scattered Ways and New Monks

Sometimes it is in those moments when present life seems most fragile that we find ourselves best able to reimagine those certainties we have taken for granted. In 1935, Dietrich Bonhoeffer, whom we met in Chapter 7, had returned to his native Germany from a teaching post at Union Theological Seminary in the USA. He did so precisely because he could see the approaching crisis for his homeland, and felt he should share it with his own people. Unlike many others, especially in the church, he could see the threat which National Socialism posed to the work of the kingdom of God. Writing to his brother, Karl, he described how he thought things might have to change in a world after the Nazi storm had swept through and overturned everything: 'The restoration of the church will surely come only from a new type of monasticism which has nothing in common with the old but a complete lack of compromise in a life lived in accordance with the Sermon on the Mount in the discipleship of Christ.'[1]

In the short term he would put this into practice in the training seminaries he founded for the 'confessing church' in Finkenwalde and Sigurdshof. In these places, constantly under threat of exposure and destruction by the Gestapo, students learned the rhythms and challenges of community life in a way which was alien to their Lutheran upbringing. They learned the value of spending quiet times, on their own, before God – with no expectation to prepare sermons, but rather to listen as sinners. They developed a strong sense of brotherhood, born out of adversity and forged under threat. Their theology was sharpened on the steel of each other's questions and it grew through companionship and prayer. Those who survived went on to lead the church with grace and strength.

It was to be decades before Bonhoeffer's concepts of 'new monasticism' truly came to fruition. When they did, it was far from the Black Forest and the dark days of oppression where they had been born.

Birth of New Monasticism

In fact, Bonhoeffer's 'new monasticism' was to be born in the British Isles. Christian witness in those islands had originally been carried there by those whose inspiration lay in the desert monastic communities of antiquity. The spiritual descendants of those desert monks were those who found their way in later centuries to the shores of the British Isles. The 'Celtic' communities in Wales, Ireland, parts of England and later Scotland were established between the fifth and twelfth centuries, and were places of rich spiritual community, prayerful stewardship of the created order, and mission. In their heyday they were great hubs of spiritual focus and prayer, bound by a rich community spirit and a wholesome attitude to the earth. They encouraged a life of prayer and industry, and felt a strong call to mission. However, the passage of the years and numerous political changes within the

Christian church would eventually undermine such a way of being. Over the centuries these communities dwindled to a few isolated places of retreat on the edges of the British mainland.

It was during the Church of England's 'Decade of Evangelism' in the 1990s that some started looking to these early Celtic roots for inspiration. What was it that they had which we could recover? How could their insights on integral mission and incarnate presence serve much later generations? One of the features of Celtic monasticism had been the 'skete', rather than the completely isolated and enclosed community. In a 'skete' the members of the community lived in close proximity but in their own homes, and pursued their own daily work while also adhering to a rhythm of prayer and a rule of life. When the Community of Aidan and Hilda was founded in 1994 it was a development of this understanding, and sought to find ways in which those living far apart could nonetheless recapture some of the benefits of those early communities. In his book *Exploring Celtic Christianity*, Ray Simpson puts it like this: 'In order to fulfil these aims the Community seeks to: research the first Celtic mission and its application today; to restore, where it is helpful, its memory and experience; resource members and churches with worship patterns and study programmes and retreats.'[2]

The Community of Aidan and Hilda would prove to be one of the first of many such communities. It now exists across many continents, and other similar organizations have sprung up elsewhere. Some are even re-examining the concept of the skete as a missional tool, with several families from a new monastic order moving into a given area, living their daily lives while bound together by covenant, and working their way towards establishing a place of worship.

Key Concepts

There are many distillations of the concepts of new monasticism available. However, I shall concentrate here on just three: the rule of life, soul friendship, and the rhythm of prayer.

Rule of life

With God's people uprooted from their time as slaves and travelling across the desert to form a new civilization in a land they had never seen, the need for rules to live by was acute. Not only that, but habits formed while living as nomads would serve them ill once they were settled in houses with land to farm and neighbours alongside them. It is for this reason that the Ten Commandments were handed down early on in the journey. They were then restated just on the brink of entering the promised land. They started with governing people's attitudes to God, but went on to cover the marital home, parents and children, truth-telling and possessions, and even the inner life of the mind. This was a comprehensive rule of life.

Christ then restated this rule for the era of the New Covenant by his 'sermon on the mount'. With every repetition of the phrase 'it is written' he was affirming and developing the rule of life as already laid down. From him, Paul would pick up the baton and carry it further. With the fledgling church springing up in all corners of the pagan empire, guidance was needed on how to maintain a distinctive identity within a hostile environment.

When the monastic orders were founded, they were all governed by a strict rule of life. This covered everything from what should be worn to table manners, diet, timetable and speech. It is tempting to think that the 'habit' is what set monks apart. In fact, it was habits, rather than habit, which typified them. The rule of life was intended to guide both soul and body into the authentic and unquestioning service of God. Even in what appear to be its harsher elements, the intention was wholesome. A good example of this would be the so-called 'Irish Penitentials' from the sixth century, with their catalogues of sins and the relevant penitence which should be performed to assuage them. In fact, this was an attempt to ensure that the response to sin and guilt was in some way proportionate rather than arbitrary. The rule of life was intended to help people live a truly spiritual life.

'New monastic' orders, such as the Order of Mission, and the 24/7 Prayer movement, also espouse a rule of life. Their members, though scattered, adhere to a code of conduct which is intended to foster and protect a constant focus on God even in the midst of daily living. In the Community of Aidan and Hilda, for instance, it includes elements such as the 'celebration and care of creation' and 'cultivating unity', as well as the elements you might expect about prayer and simplicity.[3]

Soul friendship

St Brigid once said that a 'person without a soul friend is a like a body without a head'.[4] Soul friendship is a relationship held together by a specifically spiritual agenda where the more senior brings the best out of the more junior and helps them to focus on God. A good example of this from ancient times would be St Hilda with the English poet Caedmon. He went to Hilda saying that he had had a dream where he was asked to sing. Not only did she bid him to do it there and then, but she set him 'homework' – giving him a biblical story and asking him to make a song about it. As a soul friend her focus was on his wellbeing and spiritual development. The resulting hymn has a rare beauty to it:

Now let me praise the keeper of Heaven's kingdom,
the might of the Creator, and his thought,
the work of the Father of glory, how each of wonders
the Eternal Lord established in the beginning.
He first created for the sons of men
Heaven as a roof, the holy Creator,
then Middle-earth the keeper of mankind,
the Eternal Lord, afterwards made,
the earth for men, the Almighty Lord.[5]

In the Bible we see good examples of soul friendship between Christ and his disciples. Rather than simply 'accompanying' them, he seeks to bring out the best in them – by listening, challenging and reiterating. Consider, for example, how he puts them on the spot when the five thousand must be fed. 'They do not need to go away. You give them something to eat' (Matthew 14:16). This is a calculated risk, but it teaches them a valuable lesson about trusting in him and expecting the impossible. Paul exercises soul friendship too, with people like Silas and John Mark. With the latter, as we have seen, this was not a smooth course, but it led both to grow in grace.

Monastic communities, for all their equality under God, nonetheless had a clearly defined hierarchy. Novices had their soul friends, monks had theirs, and abbots had theirs too. For each monk to have his confessor was rather like a modern counsellor having their supervisor – an insurance policy and a route to growth.

New monastic communities do not live in gathered communities, and therefore soul friendship must happen in other ways. Sometimes a person will travel to meet up with their soul friend, but they may just as often meet over Skype. The value of such a precious strand to spiritual life cannot be lost through something as surmountable as distance. Those who espouse the principles of new monasticism treat their soul-friendship relationship very seriously, ensuring that they never miss an appointment. However, they will have no hesitation about that meeting happening across continents or time zones.

Rhythm of prayer

The monastic life is set around a rhythm of prayer, with services for prayer several times each day. Those living by the Benedictine Rule, for example, would expect to gather for prayer at midnight, 6 a.m., 9 a.m., 12 noon, 3 p.m., 6 p.m. and 9 p.m. In setting up such a rule, Benedict (and others) was inspired by scriptural guidance on the regularity of prayer. The Shema, or statement of key Jewish beliefs, was to be recited every day on rising and retiring:

> Hear, O Israel: the LORD our God, the LORD is one. Love the LORD your God with all your heart and with all your soul and with all your strength. These commandments that I give you today are to be on your hearts. Impress them on your children. Talk about them when you sit at home and when you walk along the road, when you lie down and when you get up (Deuteronomy 6:4–7).

In the Sermon on the Mount Christ encourages regular prayer, and Paul urges the Christian believers in Thessalonica to 'pray without ceasing' (1 Thessalonians 5:17 ESV). In the first-century Christian writing known as the *Didache*, believers are reminded of the Lord's Prayer and told: 'Thrice in the day thus pray.'[6]

In the new monastic movements, adherents in scattered locations make a solemn pledge to pray at the same time as others in the movement each day. In the Northumbria Community, for example, this is a promise to pray morning, noon and night. The Community of Aidan and Hilda advocates the use each day of prayers at morning, midday, evening and night. Since the scattered members of the community cannot gather for prayer as such, they nonetheless draw strength from the knowledge that others are praying, out of sight, at exactly the same time.

The heart of the new monastic movement has been to 'translate' the benefits of the gathered community into a scattered existence. People longing to embed their spirituality and to draw strength from the communal life, but unable to seclude themselves away from society, have found this to be just the spiritual 'recipe' for which they are looking.

A Journey for Scattered Pilgrims?

This is just the point at which the 'pilgrimage as metaphor' concept may come home to roost. Nancy Louise Frey comments that 'pilgrims often express the desire to bring the Camino home by translating the "life is a pilgrimage" metaphor into their own lives'.[7] However, she also notes that those who seem best able to do so are so-called 'part-time pilgrims'.[8] A part-time pilgrim is someone who completes the pilgrimage in several sections over many years, rather than doing it all in one go. Thus a part-time pilgrim may return to the Way four times in as many years, rather than taking a whole month to complete the journey in one go. It has been noted by Frey that it is these people who seem better able to internalize the lessons they have learned. All those things we have examined about leaving home, provisions, communication, companions, distraction and journey's end may be better remembered if they are part of a repeating cycle rather than a once-in-a lifetime experience. Part-time pilgrims are obliged to live out those lessons in the ordinariness of life, rather than consigning them to a distant memory as a spiritual highlight. In the language of new monasticism they are to become 'contemplatives in the marketplace'.[9]

As we have seen, new monastic communities are scattered, not gathered. They are far, not near. They maintain their disciplined life across great distances and rarely get the opportunity to worship or pray face to face. In other words, they 'translate' the disciplines and understandings of an old spirituality by mapping them onto a new social reality. Perhaps there could be a model here for echoing the pilgrim's footsteps on the pavement, and answering the call of the Camino in the call centre? Simon Reed, from the Community of Aidan and Hilda, certainly thinks so: 'Pilgrimage is the focussing in a specialized way of the journey of life.'[10]

If the church historically found pilgrimage worthwhile and if a spiritual renaissance beyond the church's walls is rediscovering it all over again, we should not lightly dismiss it. Just as new monasticism has embraced the benefits of a closed religious life in an open society, so we should maybe explore the blessings of the road when we are stationary.

New monasticism is spreading, and in Norway, for example, new pilgrimage routes are opening up as it does so. What I am calling for here, though, is something more radical than simply founding new pilgrimage routes. Rather, it is a case of walking the old familiar routes – from house to shop to work and back again – with new footsteps. Asked by somebody while compiling this book where I had actually been in pilgrimage, I replied, 'Everywhere and nowhere.' It was not intended as a 'clever' answer so much as an attempt at the truth. Like Nancy Frey's part-time pilgrims, forever translating between the Camino and the commute and back again, maybe we could do the same? Careful study of the key elements we have considered in this book and a resolution to find them on the ordinary road as opposed to the old pilgrim paths could bring about something of a revolution. Like the members of new monastic communities keeping an eye out for each other's souls even when apart, or praying together without ever meeting, we could become a new kind of pilgrim altogether. This is a pilgrimage on which every Christian could join, even where physical limitations or other commitments make leaving home on an extended pilgrimage an impossibility.

What would they be like, these new pilgrims? Once, when I was speaking to a member of a new monastic order, he described a gathering at Lambeth Palace with members of the older traditional orders in cowls while he was in jeans. To his great delight, he was treated by them as being every bit as authentic despite the differences in appearance. So, what would set them apart – our incognito pilgrims?

For a start, they would have a clear sense that they were on a journey. Like the long-distance traveller, they would reflect from time to time on the home and habits which they had left behind. Not only that, but the constant call of their final destination would prevent the past from dragging them back where they did not want to go. When the journey seems slow, or the delays interminable, when home is obscured by distance and journey's end is too far away to even imagine, they would whisper to themselves these four words, 'I am a pilgrim', and set their face forwards once again. This moment of revelation might come in all kinds of places – from a pew in a church to the last spare seat on the rush-hour train – but come it will.

From time to time they will look around at their fellow Christians and note how different they are. Their voices do not sound like mine, their habits are not ones I would choose and, every once in a while, I find them every bit as irksome as they find me. As a pilgrim, though, I remember that they share my calling. We are on the same journey, nudged from our cosy nests by the same distant call of heaven. Along the way I will sometimes need to lean upon their shoulder, and they sometimes upon mine. Occasionally they will need to tug at my elbow when I am tempted to abandon the way, and sometimes I will need to wait for them at the roadside while they take a breather. The things which we would find enervating if we lived in the same place together seem somehow more tolerable on the road. After all, this companionship is only temporary – an alliance born out of the circumstances of the road. When we reach journey's end the crowd will be far bigger and the stimulus unimaginably greater, but for now we walk together in the groups, both large and small, to which we have been called.

From time to time these secret pilgrims will take stock of their possessions. Knowing that the road is long and the gradients unpredictable, they will ask whether all this stuff is really necessary. Travelling, as they do, through a land of acquisitiveness, where affluenza often seems to afflict the inhabitants, they will question all those things which they carry with them. Do they really provide the comfort, or protection or shelter, which the man in the shop said they would? Perhaps they are burdens more than assets, and would better be left at the side of the road.

When these secret pilgrims find that journey's end hoves into sight they will point it out to each other instead of looking the other way. They will remember, like the imprint of a forgotten childhood moment, that this is where they were heading all along. It will not seem so strange, or foreboding or dark, as they might have imagined. Rather, their spirits will soar at the prospect of it and they will urge each other on. When at last one or another walks through the city gate into the city, the others will wave fondly, knowing that the footsore pilgrim is home, and that their turn will come when the time is right.

For Reflection

1. Is it possible to live a covenanted community life even when scattered, do you think?
2. If you had to describe your 'rule of life' as a Christian, what would it be?
3. How do you go about maintaining a rhythm of prayer in your daily life?
4. How and where have you expressed soul friendship to another?

Around the Campfire by Max Ellis

11

Around the Campfire

Towards the end of his journey along the Camino to Santiago, journalist Jack Hitt found himself savouring a kind of mellow shared humanity in a way that he had never done before. His last night before entering the city was spent camping in a field with many others, some of whom he had met along the route and others who were strangers. Here this hard-nosed journalist waxes lyrical as he recalls the experience: 'After suffering and hazards and quarrels they found in a thing as plain as an apple or a piece of bread awe, humility and mystery.'[1] Around the campfires in that field people from all kinds of nationality, background and social status saw each other differently across the dancing flames. Shaped by the journey, like stones rolled around and around in the sea to make them smooth, they sat as equals, telling their tales and sharing their experiences.

In these next few pages, I have assembled just such a group. They come from different church backgrounds and nationalities. In fact, some have come from different centuries. In their different ways they tell their tales of the journey and what it has taught them.

- **Aymeric Picaud**. Aymeric was a monk and scholar from the town of Parthenay in the Poitou-Charentes region of western France. The town stands on one of the key routes through France for pilgrims on their way to Santiago de Compostela, and its main fortified gate is named after St James. At some point between 1135 and 1139 Aymeric is believed to have made the journey to Santiago de Compostela. His account of it was then bound into a volume with various other tales and named after Pope Calixtus II. As we noted in Chapter 5, the volume also contains manuscripts of the earliest polyphonic songs in Europe, many of them dedicated to St James. This may be evidence that pilgrims on this journey of faith first learned here to combine the different tones of their voices into a single musical whole. Even as people joined the pilgrim throng from different points before converging on the city, so here their voices blend as one. Picaud himself is often depicted as a slightly portly, bearded monk. He is rather given to dismissive descriptions of others, such as his declaration that 'the Navarese are condemned by all right-minded people'.[2]

- **Dean**. An Australian radio presenter, Dean also works with a families' charity. In 2013 he joined fellow Australian radio presenter Sheridan Voysey on a walking pilgrimage from Lindisfarne to Durham, where the Lindisfarne Gospels were on display at the time. The pilgrimage took six days, and the whole thing was billed as a 'digital' pilgrimage, with tweets and Instagram photos on the way round, and video blogs uploaded each night.

- **Sue**. Sue heads up the Methodist Diaconal order, and is a seasoned pilgrim, having completed the Camino de Santiago on two separate occasions. The first time, she did the whole thing on foot. On her second visit she was accompanied by her mother in a camper van. Her mother was battling lung cancer at the time, and the Camino was on her 'bucket list'. She now has her *compostela*.

- **Margery Kempe**. Margery was born somewhere near Norwich in around 1370. After giving birth to fourteen children and helping to provide for them by running a brewery, she gave herself to a life of pilgrimage and devotion. Over the years, she criss-crossed Europe to Italy, Spain and France, as well as visiting Jerusalem. Her autobiography, said to be the first in the English language, was discovered by chance in the early 1930s. She is often depicted dressed from head to foot in white.

- **Penelope**. An ordained priest, Penelope moved from a busy parish in London to found a retreat centre in Wiltshire. Over the years, she has led numerous pilgrimages in the United Kingdom and Tuscany, and is a spiritual director.

- **Geoffrey Chaucer**. Born in 1343, and variously serving as a page, a customs man, a Member of Parliament and a judge, Chaucer is usually depicted with a beard and a somewhat sardonic expression. Sometime between 1387 and 1400 he wrote the *Canterbury Tales*, a selection of stories by pilgrims on their way to Canterbury. Originally the work was meant to include one tale on the way there and one on the way back, but the author died without completing it.

With the fire burning up nicely, our ragtag collection of travellers sit back, hands cupped round a hot drink and the glow of the flames illuminating their different faces. Some are deeply lined, as if the journey has aged them. Others have a kind of radiance, as if the days on the road in sun, rain, wind and shade have somehow opened every pore and made them more truly alive. With the journey so nearly at an end, thoughts begin to turn to why they embarked on it in the first place.

With a coarse chuckle, Chaucer rocks back where he sits and says that it is just something you do when the season is right: 'Thanne longen folk to goon on pilgrimages, / And palmeres for to seken straunge strondes, / To ferne halwes, kowthe in sondry londes; / And specially from every shires ende / Of Engelond to Caunterbury they wende . . .'

Margery Kempe looks a little shocked and recalls her many journeys to and fro, often in fear for her life. She remembers the companions who refused to walk with her because she wept too much, and the odd strangers who fed and protected her. 'When I was commanded to go,' she says, 'I could in no way withstand it.' Nodding at her across the fire, and across the centuries, Sue nods with a kind of recognition. 'The Camino got under my skin in a way not dissimilar to my call to ordained ministry,' she says. As Margery nods, encouraging her, she continues, 'It became an itch that I just had to scratch, it just would not leave me alone, so I thought why not?' A little further round the circle, Penelope has been listening and thinking before she speaks. 'There is something inexplicably wonderful and special about walking,' she says, going on to describe it as an 'intentional stepping out', a 'leaving behind' and a 'long walk with God – intentionally wanting to find him'. Chaucer looks wistful now, the scepticism all gone, as if he would like to write a different kind of tale altogether. Picaud remembers the latter part of his journey and talks about his first glimpse of the shrine of St James in Santiago: 'divinely illuminated by paradisiac carbuncles, constantly honoured by divine fragrances, radiant in the light of celestial candles and devoutly attended by watching angels'. It is as if for him such an experience were reason enough to go. Dean nods at all that he has heard and confesses that he embarked on a pilgrimage without really understanding it fully. For him there had been a slightly wistful sense of 'walking in the footsteps of those saints of old'.

Margery chips in at this point, remembering some of the harder parts of the journeys, especially by sea. Recalling her own shipboard prayer, she looks up to the darkening sky above the fire and recites it again, as if reliving that moment: 'Show you are truly God, and no evil spirit, that has brought me here into the perils of the sea, whose counsel I have trusted and followed for many years, and shall do, through your mercy, if you deliver us from out of these grievous perils.'

Penelope looks across at her, maybe wondering if she couldn't do with a night or two at the retreat house, and recalls the ups and downs of 'walking, walking, walking, whether one feels like it or not' – blisters and rain notwithstanding. She says there is a tiredness too, even when 'the pilgrimage is invigorating'. Sue remembers that 'saying yes' was the hardest thing but by no means the last challenge. Blanching slightly at the memory, she remembers how hard it was not being able to take communion in the Roman Catholic churches along the way: 'I wanted to shout at the priests, "You will bless me but you won't feed me; what kind of a gospel are you preaching here?"' The conversation dies for a minute here, the crackle and hiss of the flames filling in an awkward silence. Sue looks across at the faces as people start to look up again, and shrugs as she says, 'We are all frail human beings.'

Rubbing his meaty hands together, Chaucer looks around at these real pilgrims, recognizing how much more interesting they are than his little band of imaginary ones and asks, 'But what did you learn, friends, what did you learn?' Calling herself 'this creature' as she is wont to do, Margery says that she learned to thank God 'with all my heart', and that 'just as he had brought me to see this earthly city of Jerusalem, so he would give me grace to see the blissful city of Jerusalem above, the city of heaven'. Picaud, so full of snide remarks about the people he met on the way, recognizes that the pilgrims on this road are like those on another, less visible, one and that 'whosoever receives them and gives them hospitality has for his guest not only St James but our Lord himself'.

Sue remembers the companionship of the road, and describes the Camino as 'a country about 4 yards wide and 800 miles long with a human community all working together'. 'Oh yes,' nods Penelope, 'fellow pilgrims can be supportive, encouraging, profound friends – even if you have only known them a few days'. 'My patience has grown deeper too,' says Sue, remarking that she is 'sort of gentler and more gracious'. Dean nods in recognition as he recalls the miles slipping by under his feet as the banter of two professional talkers gave way to a companionable reflection. 'The human body as well as the human soul is capable of far more than we often imagine,' says Penelope, rubbing an ankle in the welcome warmth of the fire's glow.

At this point a movement catches Margery's eye, and she notices a shell tattooed on the back of Sue's hand. 'A souvenir of the Camino?' she enquires. 'Oh yes,' replies Sue, admiring the simple outline. 'Every time I look at my hands it reminds me of the journey and its lessons.' She goes on to talk about living in the moment, cutting back on what you really need, rather than what you want, and 'of course just how good God is'. Penelope remembers two of her fellow pilgrims on two different pilgrimages who each came home to a call into ordained ministry. Their call, like Sue's tattoo, has never left them.

At this point, others come in, drawn perhaps by the fire and the conversation. Richard, a minister from one of Edinburgh's historic churches, observes: 'I am now convinced that pilgrimage is the best metaphor we have for the spiritual life.' Simon has joined the circle too. Simon is a priest, an incognito monk and an occasional mountaineer. As he has listened in to the conversation he talks about learning to lead a 'God-guided journey' as some of the great Celtic missionaries had done in their little boats and on their long walks.

Look a little beyond the flames and you will see some of the others who have joined us on this journey. There is Max, camera slung round his neck and fine-nibbed pen in his hand. He joined the journey out of a desire to be part of something creative. Next to him is Rachel, whose fine pen-work brings Chapter 8 to life. Beside her is Ash – a man whose life has been a journey to the brink and back again. Now there is a restlessness to his art, and the figures he has drawn for Chapters 6 and 7 seem caught as if just on the point of leaving the page and moving on elsewhere. Sitting beside him is Maureen, whose haunting pictures tell the tale of rugged life on St Kilda and elsewhere. Ryan is here, too – a cartoonist whose young man leaving home near the start of the book seems uncertain about what the road will hold. Glenn is there at the edge of the little crowd; he still remembers the physical effort to haul his giant figure to its feet in the Welsh hills above the monastery of Strata Florida. Like all the artists sitting around him, he has shared his work as readily as a pilgrim will share his food on the journey. His wooden colossus now strides across the front cover, as if heading off elsewhere in pursuit of some silent but insistent call.

Beside them there is a man writing and thinking, thinking and writing. Over the years, the journey has seeped into his veins and he just can't help himself.

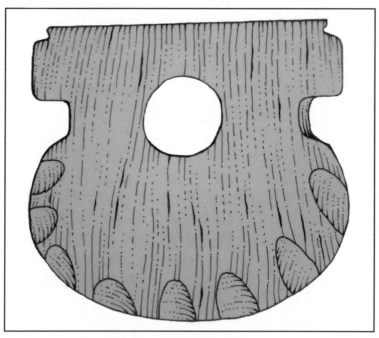

The Tale of a Shell. '2482'. Image by permission of the Winchester Excavations Committee.

12

The Tale of a Shell

Investigations for this book have led me far and wide. I have read about medieval pilgrims and contemporary adventurers. I have spent time in the company of writers who have tackled the harshest landscapes and pushed themselves right up to the limits of human endurance. I have found myself drawn into tales of contemporary pilgrimages and ancient marches of faith. To date I have visited most of these great pilgrimage sites only vicariously, through the media of word or image. I did, however, visit one pilgrimage site in Hampshire.

St Swithun was born in Winchester in 800, and served as the bishop of the city for the last ten years of his life up until 863. During his relatively short life he is credited with tutoring the future English king Alfred the Great, erecting the first ever stone bridge over the River Itchen which runs through the city, and conducting a miracle on that same structure. On one occasion a poor woman was crossing the bridge with a basket of eggs when she was jostled, dropping them all on the ground. The kindly bishop took pity, and promptly restored the smashed eggs to her, whole. After his death, Bishop Swithun was buried outside the West Door of the old Saxon church, and that might have been that.

However, when a later Bishop of Winchester, Aethelwold, expanded the church and added a Benedictine monastery, he clearly felt that a patron saint would enhance its status. Swithun's relics were dug up and enshrined in a spectacular reliquary inside the church, despite his stated wish to be buried 'out of doors, where the feet of men may pass over me'.[1] On the day that the relics were moved, 15 July 971, a storm broke out which lasted for some forty days. This gave rise to the legend that any rain on St Swithun's Day would ensure rain for forty days thereafter.

With the relics installed in the new minster, in a reliquary provide by King Edgar, Winchester's place on the 'pilgrimage trail' was assured. In its heyday it was second only to Canterbury as a site of pilgrimage within the British Isles. Pilgrims could even crawl directly underneath the reliquary in a tunnel known as the 'holy hole', bringing them as close as possible to the bones of the saint. With an even larger shrine installed in 1476, St Swithun was big business, and many pilgrims would leave offerings of gold, silver and jewellery around the casket. This went on until the reign of Henry VIII. On the night of 21 September 1538 soldiers acting on orders from the king smashed the shrine and removed all the valuables. Three years later workmen stopped up the entrance to the 'holy hole', and all trace of St Swithun's shrine was lost.

Of course many of those who had made the pilgrimage (either from Canterbury or elsewhere) to the fifteenth-century shrine were not in a position to donate gold, silver or jewellery on the completion of their pilgrimage. For the poorer pilgrim, a cheaper alternative would have to suffice. Excavations in the silt along the banks of the River Itchen in Winchester have revealed that some wore the traditional sign of St James, the scallop shell, on the pilgrimage for St Swithun. On safe arrival, some would toss their shells into the river from Swithun's bridge as an act of devotion and a thank-you for a journey safely completed.

Other pilgrim badges have been found elsewhere, and it is with the tale of one of them that I close this book. Sometime during Winchester's last century as a key pilgrimage destination, an anonymous pilgrim decided to make his way there. Either through lack of funds or unavailability, he was unable to find a scallop shell, or a more expensive metal pilgrim's badge to wear. Instead, he took a fragment of bone, readily available to hand, and fashioned it into a crude home-made version of the scallop shell. It was rough and angular and lacked all the smoothness and elegance of the real thing. However, it was his gesture of faith, and around his neck it hung for this sacred journey.

On arrival in Winchester, he went at some point to Hyde Abbey, just next to the cathedral. He may have gone there to pray, or perhaps he was seeking lodging from the community there. Whatever the reason for his visit, it was to prove the undoing of his home-made badge and at some point it fell, unnoticed, to the ground and the badge was lost. The centuries came and went, and all but a few stumps of wall of the abbey were demolished. It was not until the last decade of the twentieth century, with an archaeological dig under way before the construction of a new guildhall and visitor centre, that the little badge would see the light of day again. It was excavated, drawn, catalogued and put on display in the city museum, alongside some of its more expensive counterparts.

It was in that museum, in the summer of 2013, that I spotted that little badge and fell in love with it. I loved the way that it bore the marks of the man who had made it. I was drawn to this roughly hewn DIY version of the pilgrim's emblem. Not, for this anonymous pilgrim, a dramatic journey across the Pyrenees to Spain. Not, for him, a pilgrim's shell brought from the coast or a finely crafted emblem. Instead, for him, there was a local pilgrimage and a home-made badge. In his own way, he had made the pilgrimage his own and translated it into his own circumstances, just as this book has been urging you to do. Throughout the months of writing and research that man and his badge have been a kind of cipher to me – a shining example of what this pilgrimage business is all about. The day when I went to a dusty archaeological storehouse to see the original drawing made on site was a very special one indeed.

One day, when my journey of faith is complete, I want to meet that man. I want to shake him by the hand and feel the places where the calluses would once have been. I want to look him in the eye, thank him for making the journey his own, and tell him that I have done the same.

Resources

The St Paulinus Way – a relatively new 65-mile pilgrimage route in the United Kingdom, from Todmorden to York: http://paulinusway.blogspot.co.uk/p/paulinus-project.html

St Michael's Way – a 12.5-mile pilgrimage route across the narrower part of Cornwall: http://www.cornwalls.co.uk/walking/st_michaels_way.htm

St Cuthbert's Way – a 62-mile pilgrimage route from the Scottish Borders to the Island of Lindisfarne: http://www.stcuthbertsway.net/walk.html

The Confraternity of St James – a UK-based charity who will help you plan every step of a pilgrimage to Santiago de Compostela: http://www.csj.org.uk/

The Pilgrim Course – a teaching and discipleship course from the Church of England which encourages people to participate in the journey of faith: http://www.pilgrimcourse.org/the-course

Dying Matters – a great resource for facilitating conversations about 'journey's end': http://dyingmatters.org/

Bibliography

Anderson, Jon. 'Talking Whilst Walking: A Geographical Archaeology of Knowledge', *Area* 36.3 (2004): pp. 254–61.

Armitage, Simon. *Walking Home* (London: Faber and Faber, 2012).

Barrio Barrio, Monseñor Julián. *Guía Espiritual: Peregrinación a Santiago de Compostela* (Santiago de Compostela: Convocatoria del Año Santo, 2010).

Bede. *Ecclesiastical History of the English People* (London: Penguin, 2003).

Biddle, Martin. *Object and Economy in Medieval Winchester* (Oxford: Clarendon Press, 1990).

Bonhoeffer, Dietrich. *Life Together* (London: SCM, 2012).

Bradley, Ian. *Pilgrimage: A Spiritual and Cultural Journey* (Oxford: Lion, 2009).

Breen, Mike. *Building a Discipling Culture* (Kindle, 2011).

Bunyan, John. *A Pilgrim's Progress* (Kindle, 2013 [1678]).

Campbell, Joseph. *The Hero with a Thousand Faces* (New York: Pantheon Books, 1949).

Chan, Francis. *Who Is God? Followers' Guide* (Colorado Springs: David C. Cook, 2010).

Chaucer, Geoffrey. *The Canterbury Tales* (Kindle, 2007).

Cracknell, Linda. *Doubling Back: Ten Paths Trodden in Memory* (Glasgow: Freight, 2014).

Dawn, Maggi. *The Accidental Pilgrim* (London: Hodder, 2012).

Deam, Lisa. *A World Transformed* (Eugene, OR: Cascade Books, 2015).

Deguileville, Guillaume de. *Pilgrimage of Human Life* (1331).

Delp, Alfred. *Advent of the Heart* (San Francisco: Ignatius Press, 2006).

Frey, Nancy Louise. *On and Off the Camino* (Oakland: University of California Press, 1998).

Gerald of Wales. *The Journey through Wales / The Description of Wales* (London: Penguin, 1978).

Hitt, Jack. *Off the Road* (New York: Simon and Schuster, 2005).

Hogarth, James, ed. *The Pilgrim's Guide: A 12th Century Guide for the Pilgrim to St James of Compostela* (London: Confraternity of St James, 1996).

Kelly, Gerard. *Twitturgies* (Eastbourne: Integrity Media Europe, 2011).

Kempe, Margery. *The Book of Margery Kempe* (London: Penguin, 2005).

Koyama, Kosuke. *Three Mile an Hour God* (London: SCM, 1979).

Littledale, Richard. *Stale Bread: A Handbook for Speaking the Story* (Edinburgh: Saint Andrew Press, 2005).

Macfarlane, Robert. *Landmarks* (London: Hamish Hamilton, 2015).

— *The Old Ways: A Journey on Foot* (London: Hamish Hamilton, 2012).

— *The Wild Places* (London: Granta, 2009).

McKee, Robert. *Story: Style, Structure, Substance, and the Principles of Screenwriting* (New York: HarperCollins, 2010).

Mullen, Robert. *Call of the Camino* (Nairn: Findhorn Press, 2012).

Oppezzo, Marily and Daniel L. Schwartz. 'Give Your Ideas Some Legs: The Positive Effect of Walking on Creative Thinking', *Journal of Experimental Psychology: Learning, Memory and Cognition* 40.4 (2014): pp. 1142–52.

Palin, Michael. *Around the World in 80 Days* (London: BBC, 1990).

Reed, Simon. *Creating Community* (Abingdon: BRF, 2013).

Richards, Jeffry Jon. *War Time Preaching and Teaching* (Cambridge: Cambridge Scholars Publishing, 2009).

Ringma, Charles. *Hear the Ancient Wisdom* (London: SPCK, 2013).

Sellers, Simon and Andrew Bain. *Great Journeys: Travel the World's Most Spectacular Routes* (London: Lonely Planet, 2013).

Shinners, John. *Medieval Popular Religion, 1000–1500: A Reader*, Readings in Medieval Civilizations and Cultures (Toronto: University of Toronto Press, 2nd edn, 2006).

Simpson, Ray. *Exploring Celtic Christianity* (Stowmarket: Kevin Mayhew, 2004).

Smith, Andrew. *Moondust: The Men Who Fell to Earth* (London: Bloomsbury, 2006).

Smith, Paul. *Twitchhiker: How One Man Travelled the World by Twitter* (Chichester: Summersdale, 2010).

Solnit, Rebecca. *Wanderlust: A History of Walking* (London: Verso, 2006).

Stanford, Peter. *The Extra Mile: A 21st Century Pilgrimage* (London: Continuum, 2011).

Thomas, R.S. *Counterpoint* (Hexham: Bloodaxe, 1998).

Notes

Preface

[1] Linda Cracknell, *Doubling Back: Ten Paths Trodden in Memory* (Glasgow: Freight, 2014), loc. 54.

[2] Gerald of Wales, *The Journey through Wales / The Description of Wales* (London: Penguin, 1978), p. 178.

[3] Glenn Morris, email to the author, 13 February 2015.

1. Journey: An Introduction

[1] Frances Ridley Havergal (1836–79), 'Take my life and let it be' (1874).

[2] Jack Hitt, *Off the Road* (New York: Simon and Schuster, 2005), p. 143.

[3] Martin Luther, cited in Ian Bradley, *Pilgrimage: A Spiritual and Cultural Journey* (Oxford: Lion, 2009), p. 59.

[4] Thomas Cook https://www.thomascook.com/thomas-cook-history/ (accessed 24 Nov. 2015).

[5] Cook https://www.thomascook.com/thomas-cook-history/ (accessed 24 Nov. 2015).

[6] Kosuke Koyama, available at http://richardlittledale.me.uk/2013/05/22/ventriloquist-theology-and-the-bede/ (accessed 24 Nov. 2015).

[7] Rebecca Solnit, *Wanderlust: A History of Walking* (London: Verso, 2006), p. 5.

[8] Friedrich Nietzsche, cited in Linda Cracknell, *Doubling Back: Ten Paths Trodden in Memory* (Glasgow: Freight, 2014), loc. 54.

[9] Linda Cracknell, *Doubling Back: Ten Paths Trodden in Memory* (Glasgow: Freight, 2014), loc. 54.

[10] Peter Stanford, *The Extra Mile: A 21st Century Pilgrimage* (London: Continuum, 2011), loc. 111.

2. Leaving Home

[1] Lao Tzu; this quote is widely available online, but cited from http://www.bbc.co.uk/worldservice/learningenglish/movingwords/shortlist/laotzu.shtml (accessed 24 Nov. 2015).

[2] Cited in Richard Littledale, *Stale Bread: A Handbook for Speaking the Story* (Edinburgh: Saint Andrew Press, 2005), p. 184.

[3] Monseñor Julián Barrio Barrio, *Guía Espiritual* (Santiago de Compostela: Convocatoria del Año Santo, 2010), p. 18.

[4] http://www.206tours.com/info/elcamino/prayers.htm   (accessed 24 Nov. 2015).

3. Provisions

[1] Walter Raleigh, 'His Pilgrimage', stanza 1
http://www.bartleby.com/101/77.html (accessed 24 Nov. 2015).

[2] http://www.206tours.com/info/elcamino/prayers.htm   (accessed 24 Nov. 2015).

[3] St John Chrysostom, cited in Robert Mullen, *Call of the Camino* (Nairn: Findhorn Press, 2010), p. 81.

[4] Kosuke Koyama, *Three Mile an Hour God* (London: SCM, 1979).

[5] Nancy Louise Frey, *On and Off the Camino* (Oakland: University of California Press, 1998), p. 62.

4. Communications

[1] Ellen MacArthur http://news.bbc.co.uk/sport1/hi/other_sports/sailing/4246831.stm (accessed 24 Nov. 2015).

[2] Attributed to Dorothy Frances Gurney. See http://www.theotherpages.org/poems/gurney01.html (accessed 24 Nov. 2015).

[3] Paul Smith, *Twitchhiker: How One Man Travelled the World by Twitter* (Chichester: Summersdale, 2010), p. 330.

[4] Rebecca Solnit, *Wanderlust: A History of Walking* (London: Verso, 2006), p. 290.

[5] Solnit, *Wanderlust*, p. 45.

[6] Jon Anderson, 'Talking Whilst Walking: A Geographical Archaeology of Knowledge', *Area* 36.3 (2004): p. 260.

[7] Anderson, 'Talking Whilst Walking', p. 260.

[8] Robert Macfarlane, *The Old Ways: A Journey on Foot* (London: Hamish Hamilton, 2012), p. 24.

[9] Solnit, *Wanderlust*, p. 5.

[10] Wayne Muller https://blueskiesandlollipops.wordpress.com/tag/wayne-muller/ (accessed 24 Nov. 2015).

[11] Marily Oppezzo and Daniel Schwartz, 'Give Your Ideas Some Legs: The Positive Effect of Walking on Creative Thinking', *Journal of Experimental Psychology: Learning, Memory and Cognition* 40.4 (2014): p. 1148.

[12] Oppezzo and Schwartz, 'Give Your Ideas Some Legs', p. 1149.

[13] Robert Mullen, *The Call of the Camino* (Nairn: Findhorn Press, 2012), loc. 611.

[14] Richard Colpus, email to the author, 23 February 2015.

[15] Simon Reed https://www.aidanandhilda.org.uk/downloads/FlameAndStruggle.pdf (accessed 25 Nov. 2015).

[16] Nancy Louise Frey, *On and Off the Camino* (Oakland: University of California Press, 1998), p. 220.

5. Companions

[1] Notes sent to the author by Icon Film Distribution UK.

[2] Notes sent to the author by Icon Film Distribution UK.

3   Joseph Campbell, *The Hero with a Thousand Faces* (New York: Pantheon Books, 1949).

4   Geoffrey Chaucer, *The Canterbury Tales in Plain and Simple English*, BookCaps Study Guides (2012), p. 28.

5   St Brendan; this quote is widely available online; cited from https://www.freshexpressions.org.uk/guide/worship/blessings-medium (accessed 24 Nov. 2015).

6   St Brendan; widely available online; cited from http://incarnatus.blogspot.co.uk/2006/05/st-brendan-navigator.html (accessed 24 Nov. 2015).

7   Margery Kempe, *The Book of Margery Kempe* (London: Penguin, 2005), loc. 1545.

8   Jack Hitt, *Off the Road* (New York: Simon and Schuster, 2005), p. 137.

9   Robert Mullen, *Call of the Camino* (Nairn: Findhorn Press, 2012), loc. 2869.

10 Lisa Deam, *A World Transformed* (Oregon: Cascade, 2015), loc. 1165.

11 Swanwick Declaration, 4 September 1987 https://ctbi.org.uk/swanwick-declaration/ (accessed 24 Nov. 2015).

12 Swanwick Declaration https://ctbi.org.uk/swanwick-declaration/ (accessed 24 Nov. 2015).

13 John Fawcett (1739–1817), 'Blest be the tie that binds' (1782), stanzas 2 and 3.

6. Distractions

1   Guillaume de Deguileville, *Pilgrimage of Human Life* (1331), cited in John Shinners, *Medieval Popular Religion, 1000–1500: A Reader*, Readings in Medieval Civilizations and Cultures (Toronto: University of Toronto Press, 2nd edn, 2006), p. 316.

2   Aymeric Picaud, cited in *The Pilgrim's Guide: A 12th Century Guide for the Pilgrim to St James of Compostela* (ed. James Hogarth; London: Confraternity of St James, 1996), p. 14.

[3] Simon Armitage, *Walking Home* (London: Faber and Faber, 2012), p. 200.

[4] Peter Stanford, *The Extra Mile: A 21st Century Pilgrimage* (London: Continuum, 2011), loc. 1921.

[5] Robert Macfarlane, *The Old Ways: A Journey on Foot* (London: Hamish Hamilton, 2012), p. 14.

7. Journey's End

[1] Aymeric Picaud, cited in *The Pilgrim's Guide: A 12th Century Guide for the Pilgrim to St James of Compostela* (ed. James Hogarth; London: Confraternity of St James, 1996), p. 20.

[2] Codex Calistinus, ch. VII http://www.codexcalixtinusfacsimil. com/2012/07/the-english-version-of-book-v-codex.html (accessed 24 Nov. 2015).

[3] Picaud, *The Pilgrim's Guide*, p. 70.

[4] Jack Hitt, *Off the Road* (New York: Simon and Schuster, 2005), p. 238.

[5] William Walsham How (1823–97), 'For all the saints, who from their labours rest' (1864), stanza 4.

[6] Mark Galli and Ted Olsen, eds, *131 Christians Everyone Should Know* (Nashville: Broadman & Holman Publishers, 2000), Dietrich Bonhoeffer.

[7] Alfred Delp, *Advent of the Heart* (San Francisco: Ignatius Press, 2006), loc. 516.

[8] Delp, *Advent of the Heart*, loc. 433.

[9] Evangeline Paterson (1928–2000). Her daughter granted permission for the use of this poem. It has not been possible to ascertain whether it was ever published.

[10] Henry Scott Holland, 'The King of Terrors', sermon preached in St Paul's Cathedral, London, Sunday 15 May 1910 https://en. wikisource.org/wiki/The_King_of_Terrors (accessed 24 Nov. 2015).

[11] Scott Holland, 'The King of Terrors'.

[12] http://deathcafe.com/what/ (accessed 24 Nov. 2015).

8. A Pilgrimage Lived

[1]   Nancy Louise Frey, *On and Off the Camino* (Oakland: University of California Press, 1998), p. 178.

[2]   Andrew Smith, *Moondust: The Men Who Fell to Earth* (London: Bloomsbury, 2006), p. 347.

[3]   Martin Luther King Jr, speech delivered at the Lincoln Memorial, Washington DC, 28 August 1963 http://www.americanrhetoric.com/speeches/mlkihaveadream.htm (accessed 24 Nov. 2015).

[4]   Robert Macfarlane, *The Old Ways: A Journey on Foot* (London: Hamish Hamilton, 2012), p. 26.

[5]   Francis Chan, *Who Is God? Followers' Guide* (Colorado Springs: David C. Cook, 2010), p. 68.

[6]   Michael Palin, *Around the World in 80 Days* (London: BBC, 1990), p. 85.

9. The Language of the Road

[1]   Quoted in Robert Macfarlane, *Landmarks* (London: Hamish Hamilton, 2015), loc. 331.

[2]   Macfarlane, *Landmarks*, loc. 360.

[3]   Jack Hitt, *Off the Road* (New York: Simon and Schuster, 2005), p. 177.

[4]   http://www.elcaminosantiago.com/PDF/Ultreia.pdf (accessed 24 Nov. 2015).

10. Scattered Ways and New Monks

[1]   Dietrich Bonhoeffer, letter to Karl Friedrich Bonhoeffer, 14 January 1935; cited in Jeffrey Jon Richards, *War Time Preaching and Teaching* (Cambridge: Cambridge Scholars Publishing, 2009), p. 154.

[2]   Ray Simpson, *Exploring Celtic Christianity* (Stowmarket: Kevin Mayhew, 2004), p. 30.

3 https://www.aidanandhilda.org.uk/about-way.php (accessed 25 Nov. 2015).

4 St Brigid (*c.*451–525), cited from http://www.explorefaith.org/livingspiritually/following_a_sacred_path/celtic_christianity/soul_friends.php (accessed 25 Nov. 2015).

5 Caedmon, *Caedmon's Hymn*, lines 1 and 2; http://www.songandpraise.org/caedmons-hymn.htm (accessed 24 Nov. 2015).

6 *Didache*, Section VIII, line 3 http://www.thedidache.com/ (accessed 25 Nov. 2015).

7 Nancy Louise Frey, *On and Off the Camino* (Oakland: University of California Press, 1998), p. 202.

8 Frey, *On and Off the Camino*, p. 215.

9 Simon Reed, joint Guardian of the Community of Aidan and Hilda.

10 Reed, conversation with the author, March 2015.

11. Around the Campfire

1 Jack Hitt, *Off the Road* (New York: Simon and Schuster, 2005), p. 238.

2 Aymeric Picaud, cited in *The Pilgrim's Guide: A 12th Century Guide for the Pilgrim to St James of Compostela* (ed. James Hogarth; London: Confraternity of St James, 1996), p. 184.

12. The Tale of a Shell

1 St Swithun http://www.winchester-cathedral.org.uk/our-heritage/famous-people/st-swithun/ (accessed 25 Nov. 2015).

Authentic

We trust you enjoyed reading this book
from Authentic. If you want to be informed
of any new titles from this author and other
releases you can sign up to the Authentic
newsletter by contacting us:

By post:
Authentic Media Limited
PO Box 6326
Bletchley
Milton Keynes
MK1 9GG

E-mail:
info@authenticmedia.co.uk

Follow us: